Why I Left America and Other Essays

Why I Left America
and Other Essays

By

Oliver W. Harrington

Edited, with an Introduction, by

M. Thomas Inge

University Press of Mississippi
Jackson

These essays appeared originally in the following publications and are reprinted here with permission:

"The Last Days of Richard Wright," *Ebony*, 16 (February 1961), 83–86, 88, 90, 92–94.

"The Mysterious Death of Richard Wright," *Daily World*, 17 December 1977, Magazine, M4–M5.

"How Bootsie Was Born," *Freedomways*, 3 (1963), 518–524.

"Our Beloved Pauli," *Freedomways*, 11 (1971), 58–63.

"Look Homeward Baby," *Freedomways*, 13 (1973), 135–143, 200–215.

"Through Black Eyes," *Freedomways*, 14 (1974), 154–157.

"Like Most of Us Kids," *Freedomways*, 16 (1976), 255–257.

Where is the Justice? Detroit: Walter O. Evans, 1991.

Why I Left America. Detroit: Walter O. Evans, 1991.

Essays copyright © 1993 by Oliver W. Harrington
Introduction copyright © 1993 by M. Thomas Inge
All rights reserved
Manufactured in the United States of America
Designed by Sally Hamlin

96   95   94   4   3   2   1

The paper in this book meets the guidelines for permanence and durability of the Committee on Production Guidelines for Book Longevity of the Council on Library Resources.

Library of Congress Cataloging-in-Publication Data

Harrington, Oliver, 1913–
    Why I left America and other essays / by Oliver W. Harrington ;
    edited with an introduction by M. Thomas Inge.
        p.   cm.
    Includes index.
    ISBN 0-87805-655-6—ISBN 0-87805-739-0 (pbk)
    1. Harrington, Oliver, 1913–   .   2. Afro-American artists—
Biography.   3. Expatriate artists—France—Paris.   4. Expatriate
artists—Germany—Berlin.   I. Inge, M. Thomas.   II. Title.
N6537.H349A2   1993
741.5′092—dc20
[B]   93-25039
                                                                                  CIP

British Library Cataloging-in-Publication data available

To

Nonnie

Olivia

and

Ollie,

Jr.

Contents

Foreword

A Friendship Revisited

The lives of great men are forsaken
paths overgrown by brambles.
Rainer Maria Rilke

One of Richard Wright's biographers recently commented that Dick Wright was unable to keep his friends for very long. My memories of growing up in my father's house beg to differ. Once Dick's elaborate mechanisms of defence were disarmed—his armour had after all enabled him to survive in the American South of his childhood—he could invest in his friendships in a rare and delightful way. To paraphrase La Rochefoucauld, friendship, real friendship, has something in common with ghosts: everybody talks about them but nobody has actually seen any. But I believe that as children we also grow and thrive on the affective soil of our parents' ability to form solid friendships. Not only because they are exemplary but because they nurture our belief in the possibility of trust—and trust has been a rare commodity amongst us African-Americans since the trauma of betrayal we experienced as slaves.

The friendship between Ollie Harrington, former NAACP public relations officer, former war correspondent, artist and cartoonist, and Richard Wright, the novelist, activist and essayist, did just that for me: it caused me to reach back unconsciously to what the experience of an extended family might have been before the Crossing. Ollie was always "around" in the African sense of the term. Ollie's presence by my father's side was part of my growing up sane in what my father later called an "island of hallucination." It was part of my early social bonding and my belief in the endurance of trust and loyalty in an exiled black community where betrayal and the darkness of suspicion bred by McCarthyism, the cold war, and enduring racism did not exactly constitute a training ground for brotherly love.

As Ellen Wright, my mother, once reminisced: "They were like brothers without any words being said." Their friendship ran deep, but between the lines and off the cuff. Now that I think of it, there was in the wordlessness of their bond the very quality of silence which enables laughter to bubble up and break out when I now look at Ollie's cartoons.

Richard Wright's two most important, most intellectually or artistically satisfying friendships with black male contemporaries were those which bound him to George Padmore, the West Indian panafricanist and writer, and to Ollie Harrington. George Padmore died in September 1959, a year before Dick did. After that Ollie became Dick's "last, best friend" to quote Margaret Walker's inscription on the copy of her book she sent Ollie in Berlin. Between the three of them, they summed up in a complementary way three fascinating ways of dealing with the contradiction between cold war and creativity, the dialectics of race and panafricanism, of politics and power. They all three endear themselves to me for the inimitable way they have stood aside when power politics could have ensnared them and destroyed their creativity. They are—all three of them—my intellectual and ethical mentors. The link with both Ollie and George is proof of how resolutely nonsectarian Richard Wright was in his choice of friends: Padmore had broken, as Wright had, with communism but had always eluded rightwing anti-communist co-optation; Harrington's respect for the outstanding work of Communist Party luminaries like William Patterson never led him to become a member himself. The three of them never actually—though Ollie can correct me here—met in a room but what a landmark in the history of the links between Black America, the Carribean, and Africa if they had! In any event they shared similar gifts of wit, humour, courage and a very special flair for storytelling. And Ollie is here to keep that storytelling tradition alive.

Paradoxically, Ollie is almost an "invisible man" in the major biographies on Richard Wright by Constance Webb, Michel Fabre, Addison Gayle and Margaret Walker. Not that he is totally absent from the biographical explorations of Wright's life and work as written between 1960 and today. No, he is in there but more emphasis is often given to the absence of meaningful relationship between Richard Wright and Jimmy Baldwin than to Richard Wright's very real connection with Ollie Harrington. He is present in the biographies but as a name linked almost exclusively to the Gibson-Harrington affair (1958), somehow reducing Ollie, the person and the artist, to a cardboard dummy, a target for the anti-communist provocation then aimed at him. But Ollie's place in my father's life exceeded the reluctant and unwanted publicity Richard Gibson's provocation brought him, and, indeed, if anything, Gibson's confessed forgery of Ollie's signature to inflammatory pro-communist statements on Algeria's independence reinforced the complicity element in Dick and Ollie's friendship. Perhaps now that the cold war has lost its momentum, the real place of people like Ollie will be reassessed in the history of our black artists and intellectuals. And reassessment does not mean reinstatement: Ollie does not need to be "reinstated" in the derogatory sense of that term. But in a strange sense, the black artist who left for Berlin shortly after the trauma of the suspicious death of Dick Wright, his best friend, who fell in love with and married a Berliner and watched the Wall go up between himself and the world he knew, perhaps in that sense he has also been partly "walled out" of the biographies: Ollie has hardly been interviewed between 1961 and the end of the cold war. When he was quoted it was on the basis of his articles and there were, given the times, many more quotes from his articles on Dick for *Ebony* than from his contributions to the *Daily World.* To be fair to the biographers, Ollie as a valid biographical source was far removed on the other side of a dark curtain which has also been drawn across his knowledge of key aspects of his best friend's life and death. Today, the cold war is slowly fizzling out and leaving in the thawed space of historical and biographical research exciting areas of information which will probably become food for all shades of biographical thought. Why not? History is long.

When I set out to recapture the past and write my memoir on my father in 1987, I attempted to find Ollie's whereabouts in exactly the same way as I tried to seek out my father's other peers and contemporaries. Rumour definitely had him dead. (I wonder how many other imaginary obituaries the Wall has been responsible for?) When I finally located Ollie—healthy, alive and kicking—and went to interview him in East Berlin shortly before the Wall came down, I solemnly informed him about his death since he might have missed it in the newspapers. We laughed and laughed. It was so like a story by Richard Wright. So like Cross Damon attending his own funeral in *The Outsider.* Mark Twain had foreseen it all.

Only two books that I can think of begin to do justice to Ollie's real place in Dick's life: Chester Himes's autobiography (although the gossipy and petulant undertones of some of Chester's anecdotes sometimes mar his narrative) and Richard

Wright's own last, unfinished, unpublished novel on African-American expatriates in Paris: "Island of Hallucination." The manuscript of "Island of Hallucination" is stored, sealed, in the Beinecke Library at Yale University. The reason for this is two-fold: Dick was not yet satisfied with the state of his manuscript, and, since it is a "roman à clef," it could provoke a certain amount of libel-prone fantasies about who is meant to be whom. Although to my mind, all the characters are complexly composite.

In spite of the sealed state of Richard Wright's last manuscript, I have estate permission to quote from it. So here are some of the words of wisdom uttered by one of the protagonists, Ned Harrison, a character who closely resembles Ollie Harrington. (Ned Harrison is giving advice to Fishbelly, the young, racially and politically naive hero freshly arrived in Paris from the turbulence of the American South):

> "Fish," Ned said, "our race has no memory. Each generation lives as though no one has lived before it. What my father learned from his living died with him (. . .) You can't blame your father if he died and left you poor; maybe he had no chance to control the economic forces that shaped his destiny. But, dammit, we can blame our fathers for dying and leaving us ignorant of what they encountered in life, what they felt about it. Now, Fish, it is to try to establish that continuity of experience that makes me talk to you like this."

Ned Harrison is described in "Island of Hallucination" as "fiftyish, graying at the temples, and, though heavy in body, he conveyed the impression of alert strength, of tough mental agility. The man's poise and self-possession baffled." All those who have met Ollie Harrington will recognize him in the above description but I think the portrayal of Ned Harrison in "Island of Hallucination" is more complicated. I think Ned Harrison is a composite portrayal of Richard Wright *and* Ollie Harrington—a monument to their complicity in their philosophical appraisal of the undercurrents in the African-American community of exiles in Paris during the fifties. There is in Ned Harrison the same "wisdom of distance" that only Ollie and Dick could achieve through talking it out or rather "storytelling it out" during their long sessions at the Café Tournon with the younger newly arrived exiles flocking around. Fishbelly is one of the young new arrivals. But the character, Fishbelly, is also more than that: he is their fictional and spiritual heir, the one they must pass their racial and political wisdom on to. He is their native son—what they were when they also first left the racial nightmare, new in Paris, still wound up tight with a fear they could not seem to shake off. Fishbelly is both their past as they remember it and their future as they would hope to control it. And so they school him, and through him a whole younger generation of African-Americans, in the lessons of race in exile. And isn't the experience of racism an exile in itself? Ned Harrison in "Island of Hallucination" is the highest tribute Dick Wright ever paid to his friendship with Ollie Harrington and he may well have been thinking of Ollie when he quoted Mark Twain on the title page of Book I:

> "I like him; I am ashamed of him, and it is a delight to me to be where he is if he has new material on which to work his vanities where they will show him off as with a limelight."

The wall, then, is down.

Life will not be the same again anywhere as this century ends. Ollie Harrington was welcomed in April of this year in Detroit as one of the long lost native sons he is—but also as one of America's outstanding artists, black or white. He brought the originals of his cartoons with him out of his long exile and those of us who had the privilege of seeing them again, together, as a living body of connected work, recognized the humane gentle bite of his genius. There is an unusual quality of stilled laughter in his work—mild, derisive, subterranean laughter at the corrupt ways of racism and injustice throughout the world. And it is his victory that he can laugh and make us laugh. The laughter he shares with us is illuminating, healing and promotes the best in us. His cartoons are like his friendship with Richard Wright, full of uproarious but deadly serious little stories, silver stories with black, very black linings, and with each studied, detailed stroke of his pen, he puts in such hints of warmth, tolerance, and resiliency that words suddenly falter and laughter, Ollie's special kind of laughter, takes over.

For Dick Wright and Ollie Harrington, deep emotion is not a thing you can put into words—those white words long ago imposed on us—but it is a thing you can put into laughter because laughter is a language native to the soul.

Julia Wright
Paris, August 1991

Introduction

In the books about and the memoirs of Richard Wright, Chester Himes, and the other African-American artists and intellectuals who exiled themselves to Paris after World War II, the name of Ollie Harrington appears frequently, but he is always somewhere there in the background. In his autobiography, *My Life of Absurdity*, Chester Himes identifies him as his "best friend," "the best raconteur I'd ever known," and the "accepted leader for all the blacks of the Quarter, who in turn attracted all the black Americans in the city. It was really Ollie who singlehandedly made the Café Tournon famous in the world."[1]

Michel Fabre, in *The Unfinished Quest of Richard Wright*, described Harrington as a "war correspondent, . . . a former NAACP public relations officer, and a well-known cartoonist for the Pittsburgh *Courier*."[2] In *Richard Wright: Ordeal of a Native Son*, Addison Gayle noted that when "Ollie Harrington, a one-time war correspondent and cartoonist . . . arrived at the American colony, Wright gained his most faithful and lasting friend."[3] Margaret Walker identified him as "perhaps Wright's closest friend and confidante in Europe."[4] When a writer for *Esquire* magazine set out in 1965 to find out what had happened to the "hipsters" of the 1950s, he was told to try to find Harrington, "the last hipster of them all."[5]

Despite these numerous references, Harrington has seldom been discussed in any detail, and he has remained a kind of shadow figure in American literary and cultural history. When Michel Fabre wrote his study *From Harlem to Paris: Black American Writers in France, 1840–1980*, Harrington is mentioned several times because of his connections with Wright, Himes, and others, but Fabre's decision to focus only on "creative writers" and eliminate "material on artists and musicians" again kept him in the background.[6] One of the reasons for his invisibility probably has to do with the fact that Harrington was primarily a "cartoonist" and not a writer of fiction or books of social protest. That he eventually became a writer of memoirs of keen insight and richly felt experience is demonstrated by this volume. The general lack of information about him also probably has to do with the way he has led his life largely as an expatriate.

Oliver Wendell Harrington was born in Valhalla, New York, on 14 February 1912.[7] His father came from North Carolina seeking work on the dams and reservoirs under construction, and he met there a young Jewish woman from Budapest. They married and had four children. When Oliver was seven, the family moved to the South Bronx into a racially mixed neighborhood. Here he would encounter racism for the first time. As Harrington tells the story in the last essay in this volume, one day a teacher called him and the only other black child in the class to the front of the room and pronounced them both trash that belonged in the wastebasket. While shocked and dismayed by the experience, Harrington soon turned it to a personal advantage. He began to draw caricatures of the teacher trapped in horrible circumstances, and he felt so much better by relieving his desire for revenge that he decided to become a cartoonist.

After graduating from DeWitt Clinton High School in 1929, he moved to Harlem, found a room at the YMCA, began to do odd jobs, sought out free-lance art work, and began to study at the National Academy of Design. His first published work included political cartoons for two black newspapers, *The National*

Introduction

News and the *New York State Contender*, in 1932. Harrington arrived in the community during the Harlem Renaissance and became friends with such writers as Rudolph Fisher, Wallace Thurman, Arna Bontemps, and especially Langston Hughes, who became a mentor to the aspiring young humorist and cartoonist.

Harrington soon began to receive assignments from such prestigious black newspapers as the New York *Amsterdam News*, the Pittsburgh *Courier*, and the Baltimore *Afro-American*. In March 1933, he began to draw a comic strip, at first called *Boop* and then *Scoop*, about a small child much in the tradition of such popular features as Percy Crosby's *Skippy* and Harold Gray's *Little Orphan Annie*. On 25 May 1935, he began for the *Amsterdam News* a single panel cartoon called *Dark Laughter*, which appeared alongside the contributions of such recognized black newspaper cartoonists as E. Simms Campbell and Jay Jackson. The panel was based on the humorous events and people Harrington observed in Harlem on a daily basis—and then something magical happened. Beginning on 28 December 1935, a rotund and disreputable character named Bootsie appeared for the first time. As he explains in the essay in this book, "How Bootsie Was Born," Harrington had stumbled across the character which would bring him fame. For the next thirty years, he would continue the adventures of Bootsie, an African-American wise fool and urban everyman who would reflect comically in his nature and actions on the skills, manipulations, and compromises necessary for black survival in a racist society. It was on the basis of Bootsie that Langston Hughes nominated Harrington as the premier African-American cartoonist and an unsurpassed social satirist on race relations. Hughes wrote the introduction to the 1958 anthology *Bootsie and Others*.

All the while, Harrington continued his education by attending the Yale University School of Fine Arts. Supporting himself with his newspaper cartoons, a scholarship, and odd jobs like washing dishes in a fraternity house, he finished his BFA degree in 1940. He had the pleasure of seeing one of his paintings featured in the 12 February 1940 issue of *Life* magazine, a somber work called "Deep South" which reflected the strong influence of El Greco and Thomas Hart Benton, two artists who also turned to exaggeration and caricature as ways of commenting on their subject matter.

Harrington's first full-time job came as art director of *The People's Voice*, a weekly begun by Adam Clayton Powell, Jr., on 14 February 1942. In addition to the *Dark Laughter* panel featuring Bootsie, he contributed powerful editorial cartoons, illustrations, humorous panels and features, and, for a short while, even a comic strip. He illustrated the first installments of a serialization of Richard Wright's *Native Son* beginning in the first issue, until the series was cancelled due to readers' complaints about the profanity used by Wright's characters. This was the first and only collaboration between two men who later would become the closest of friends in Paris.

By 1943, Harrington was working primarily for the Pittsburgh *Courier*, doing stories about the contributions of black soldiers to the war effort, drawing Bootsie cartoons, and providing a striking comic strip called *Jive Gray*, which began on 4 May 1943. Turning to Milton Caniff's popular *Terry and the Pirates* for stylistic cues and narrative devices, Harrington adapted Caniff's techniques of realistic rendition to his own purposes. *Jive Gray*, which ran for several years, remains one of the few adventure strips to deal effectively with the war from the black perspective. Unfortunately it has been overlooked in the histories of the American comic strip.

In January 1944, Harrington was sent abroad by the Pittsburgh *Courier* as a war correspondent. He left on a convoy with the all-black 332d Fighter Squadron, which stopped in North Africa before proceeding to Taranto, Italy, in February. His dispatches for the *Courier*, posted from Italy and France, were stories about the exploits of young black soldiers at the front, the successes of the 332d and other fighter groups, and personal essays about people he met and experiences he had on and behind the battle lines, mostly serious but occasionally humorous. In stories with such headlines as "War Has Leveling Influence on Racial Bars" (11 March 1944) and "Black, White, Red Brazilian Troops March, Socialize Freely in Naples" (5 August 1944), he commented on the extent to which combat conditions erased racial tensions and allowed for courage and skill to determine a person's worth rather than skin color. These were experiences which he hoped would extend to postwar society in America.

This was not to be the case. On his return home in December 1944, he was saddened to learn of new racial outrages in the South. As the black veterans returned to the states, they too learned that Jim Crow laws still prevailed and second-class citizenship remained the order of the day. Thus, when NAACP executive Walter White, whom he had met in Italy, asked Harrington in 1946 to organize a public relations department for the organization, he was persuaded to accept the challenge of trying to make a difference in race relations through public debate and the dissemination of information. His position led him to the podium many times. On 28 October 1946, he debated then U. S. Attorney General Tom Clark in New York on "The Struggle for Justice as a World Force" (the text of Harrington's remarks is included in this book), and on 24 November, he spoke at an NAACP youth conference in New Orleans on the rights of blacks to participate fully in both the political and cultural life of the nation (New York *Times*, 29 November 1946, p. 32).

By the end of 1947, Harrington had left the NAACP and returned to his drawing board, producing Bootsie panels and editorial and sports cartoons for the black press and illustra-

xxi

tions for books, including the award-winning drawings for a children's book, *The Runaway Elephant* by Ellen F. Tarry in 1950. His public prominence as an outspoken critic of racial injustice while with the NAACP, and his support for such left-wing political leaders as W. E. B. DuBois and Benjamin J. Davis, however, drew him to the attention of the various governmental agencies then investigating Communism and suspected subversion in America. Those were the days when the House Un-American Activities Committee and Joseph McCarthy were in full swing demolishing civil liberties and the reputations of innocent people in the name of a politically pure nation. As he recounts the story in "Why I Left America," having been warned by a friend in Army Intelligence that he was about to be investigated, Harrington left in 1951 for Paris, where he had long wanted to continue his art studies since his days at Yale.

Paris had already become a mecca for young black writers, artists, musicians, performers, and intellectuals following World War II because they found there none of the social and personal discrimination that curbed them at home. The most prominent to settle there permanently in 1946 was the major American novelist Richard Wright. Soon he was joined by such novelists as Chester Himes, William Gardner Smith, and a young James Baldwin, as well as other artists and writers. It was in the Café Tournon, where many of them gathered for afternoon coffee, that Harrington came to know Richard Wright.[8] Harrington would remain his closest friend for the remainder of Wright's life. It was Harrington, however, who soon became the center of the group because of his expert skills as a tale teller and conversationalist. As Chester Himes described the situation:

> Ollie was the center of the American community on the Left Bank in Paris, white and black, and he was the greatest Lothario in the history of the whole Latin Quarter. And he was a

fabulous raconteur too. He used to keep people spellbound for hours. So they collected there because of Ollie. Then the rest of us came.[9]

Harrington earned his living by continuing to contribute cartoons to the Pittsburgh *Courier* and the Chicago *Defender* in the States, painted at the Grande Chaumière where artists gathered to sketch and draw from live models, and pursued with vigor a rich social life with his friends, much of which is described in his essay "Look Homeward Baby" and the first essay on Richard Wright in this collection. The pleasures of this new way of life were often interrupted, however, by bureaucratic hassles from the American Embassy, which was suspicious of the politics of all the black expatriates.

Harrington also became involved in an unfortunate altercation that became known in the American community as the "Gibson affair," which Michel Fabre has described in his biography of Richard Wright:

> In 1956, Wright's friend Ollie Harrington . . . had rented his Paris studio while he was away on the Côte d'Azur to Richard Gibson, a young black novelist in Paris on a Whitney scholarship. Harrington was disagreeably surprised on his return to find that Gibson not only refused to vacate the apartment, but claimed to own the furniture, paintings and personal belongings that he had left behind. The argument continued for almost two years. Gibson made violent attacks which verged on the psychotic, while Harrington resigned himself to living elsewhere rather than call in the police, fearing that the American Embassy might intervene on account of his status as an expatriate with Communist sympathies. . . .
>
> In 1957, one of the letters to the editor of the October 21 issue of *Life* magazine bore Harrington's signature and, replying to a September 30 article, violently condemned French policy in Algeria. Similar letters were also sent to *The Observer* in London, in reply to articles by M. Kraf and John

G. Weightman that appeared on January 20 and January 30, 1958. Harrington, however, had not written these letters. Since the French policy was to deport any foreigner who got involved with French domestic politics, someone must have used this maneuver to compromise him, and he accordingly initiated an investigation with the support of the well-known criminal lawyer Jacques Mercier. Both the French and the American police found conclusive evidence that Gibson had written the letters. A memorable fight ensued in the Café de Tournon, where Harrington thrashed his opponent so thoroughly that he had to be taken to the hospital; Gibson signed a confession, but the American Embassy possibly intervened with the Sûreté Nationale to hush up the affair.[10]

Things crashed in on the Parisian idyll too when Richard Wright died quite unexpectedly and under strange circumstances. Harrington has described the events and their significance in the two essays on Wright in this volume.

Without Wright as an anchor in Paris, Harrington began to look for work elsewhere. The Aufbau Publishers in East Berlin offered him a contract to illustrate a series of translations of classic American and English literature in 1961, and after he had settled into a small hotel to do the drawings, he suddenly found himself on the wrong side of the border with the Berlin Wall going up in between. These circumstances and why he remained in East Germany are related in his essay "Why I Left America."

Publications in East Berlin were happy to employ Harrington's skills as an artist, and given his inside knowledge of American life and society, he was encouraged to contribute political cartoons with special attention to American racism, poverty, and foreign policy. The humor magazine *Eulenspiegel* and the popular general interest *Das Magazine* became the major vehicles for his cartoons, many of which were rendered in full color, a luxury he had not experienced before. Although he refused to join the Communist Party in Germany, he came to occupy a special status as a cult figure among intellectuals, professors, and students who admired his work.

In 1968, the New York *Daily World* also solicited Harrington's political cartoons, and beginning on 19 October, a series of bold and darkly satirical drawings appeared in this Communist paper which reached 72,000 readers weekly. Harrington's presence undoubtedly helped the paper achieve this circulation figure, as there were many fans of his visual commentaries who had little sympathy for the publication's politics. A selection of his cartoons from the past three decades for American and German publications may be found in *Dark Laughter: The Satiric Art of Oliver W. Harrington* (University Press of Mississippi, 1993). Except for two trips home in 1972 and 1991, Harrington has remained behind the Iron Curtain and outlasted it. In 1964, he met a journalist and economist named Helma Richter, who eventually became his wife and the mother of his son, Oliver Harrington, Jr.

How Harrington began writing these personal essays and memoirs seems more a matter of coincidence than intent. Shortly after the sudden death of Richard Wright, *Ebony* magazine cabled an offer to Harrington to commission an article about his friendship with the novelist. Although Harrington had written many newspaper articles and dispatches as a war correspondent, he had never undertaken an assignment of this nature, so Chester Himes both encouraged and helped him prepare an outline. The article appeared in the February 1961 issue of *Ebony* with seventeen photographs and a short piece by Langston Hughes, the last person to visit Wright at his home before his death.

While the essay "Last Days of Richard Wright" is largely a warm and admiring portrait of Wright's character and personality, his family life and friends in Paris, his struggles with racism and the governmental bureaucracy abroad, in the final paragraphs Harrington reported in a matter-of-fact manner on the circumstances of Wright's death. While he refrained from any explicit statement, it is clear that Harrington was not happy with the official explanation of Wright's unexpected turn for the worse. Why had not the danger of a "very sudden heart attack" been detected earlier by his attending physicians?

Harrington would express his concerns more frankly sixteen years later in an article for the New York *Daily World* published 17 December 1977, called "The Mysterious Death of Richard Wright." Here he outlined the political forces at work, the surveillance of black expatriates by the CIA and the FBI, and Wright's reawakened interest in Communism, all of which made his death appear to be a desirable thing from the point of view of the officials. Harrington simply raised questions rather than make charges, but these are the questions which have led Wright's biographers to speculate about the possibility of an arranged assassination. The matter has yet to be satisfactorily or conclusively explained.

Harrington's other essays were written for *Freedomways* magazine, and, taken together, they describe in rich detail his experiences in the States and abroad which have shaped and influenced his career as a cartoonist, a political artist, and a cultural ambassador without portfolio. He must have been frequently asked to explain how he came to create Bootsie, the comic character who brought him enduring fame in the black community. In "How Bootsie Was Born," published in *Freedomways* in 1963, he described how the falling together of the Harlem social and cultural milieu, his keen eye for local color, and his need to earn a living as a cartoonist made the birth of Bootsie almost an inevitability. He also explained how much of himself is invested in Bootsie. Among the many influential and accomplished people Harrington came to know in Harlem, one of the most admired was Paul Robeson. His second contribution to *Freedomways* in 1971, "Our Beloved Pauli," celebrates Robeson and the worldwide fame he achieved as singer, political activist, and champion of the oppressed.

Harrington's next essay, "Look Homeward Baby," appeared in two installments in *Freedomways* in 1973. In this his lengthiest piece, he continued the richly detailed remembrance of times past in Harlem characteristic of the earlier essays. Honed now by having lived out of the States for over two decades, the sarcasm against racism and the illogic of the white man in race relations became sharper and more pronounced. He moved chronologically through the war years, the aftermath of oppression to restore blacks to their prewar condition, and the settling in Paris of numerous black writers and artists after the war to experience the kinds of personal and creative freedoms impossible at home. While the humor, tall tales, and comic anecdotes continued unabated, Harrington made clear why he himself joined the exodus. The last part of the essay described how America appeared to him on his first trip home in 1972 after having left for Paris in 1951. He painted a bleak picture of a blighted landscape where things appeared to have degenerated rather than improved, but he was able still to place his faith in the young people, both black and white, who seemed able to see beyond the bigotry of the moment to a better way of life. The entire essay constitutes an autobiographical *tour de force* and a literary event of the first order.

Harrington contributed two further pieces to *Freedomways*— reviews of books by fellow artists and cartoonists Elton C. Fax and Brumsic Brandon, Jr., in 1974 and 1976. These two short essays are Harrington's only comments on the power and influence of the art form he practiced throughout his career. They are also insightful appreciations of two accomplished but neglected African-American artists.

The remaining two pieces collected in this book are basically the texts of addresses by Harrington delivered at different points in his life. "Where Is the Justice?" was presented on 28

October 1946 at the fifteenth Annual New York Herald Tribune Forum on "The Struggle for Justice as a World Force," held at the Waldorf Astoria Hotel. Harrington was then public relations director for the NAACP, and the address was a challenge to U. S. Attorney General Tom Clark also on the podium. Clark had claimed considerable progress in the investigations of lynching and racial crimes in the South. Harrington provided a forceful argument against the presence of any progress in racial justice and harmony in America and issued a warning about the inevitable consequences of denying some 15 million black Americans their constitutional rights.

The final address, "Why I Left America," was delivered on 18 April 1991, at Wayne State University on the occasion of Harrington's second return to the States in forty years under the auspices of Detroit physician and collector of African-American art and culture, Walter O. Evans. Evans has assembled the largest collection of original art by Harrington in the States, and he has mounted several one-man shows of humorous and editorial cartoons drawn by Harrington in the past three decades. "Why I Left America" ranges over the whole of Harrington's life and career, from his childhood days in the Bronx to his reasons for staying abroad in Paris and East Berlin for the largest part of his life. He repeated several anecdotes from earlier essays, but he provided new material about his experiences and reached a climax with the intriguing story of how he first became trapped behind the Iron Curtain.

All of the material assembled here constitutes a loosely organized but sensitively rendered account of what being black has meant in this century. It is an autobiography which has been missing for too long from the bookshelf of essential African-American literature and culture.

M. Thomas Inge
March 1993

Introduction

NOTES

1. Chester Himes, *My Life of Absurdity* (Garden City, NY: Doubleday, 1976), 35.

2. Michel Fabre, *The Unfinished Quest of Richard Wright* (New York: William Morrow, 1973), 297, 461.

3. Addison Gayle, *Richard Wright: Ordeal of a Native Son* (Garden City, NY: Anchor Press/Doubleday, 1980), 207.

4. Margaret Walker, *Richard Wright: Daemonic Genius* (New York: Warner Books, 1985), 184.

5. Marion Magid, "The Death of Hip," *Esquire*, 63 (June 1965), 95.

6. Michel Fabre, *From Harlem to Paris: Black American Writers in France, 1840–1980* (Urbana: University of Illinois Press, 1991), xi.

7. For a fuller biographical account, see the present writer's "Introduction" to *Dark Laughter: The Satiric Art of Oliver W. Harrington* (Jackson: University Press of Mississippi, 1993). Christine McKay of the Schomburg Center for Research in Black Culture of the New York Public Library is to be thanked for generously sharing her biographical research on Harrington.

8. A news story in the New York *Amsterdam News* on 16 December 1944, "Langston Hughes Gives An International Party," places Harrington at a party with Richard Wright shortly after his return from Italy. Harrington, however, remembers attending no such party and believes that the paper has confused two separate events and conflated the guest list. He does remember attending a party at that time given for Chester Himes. In any case, Harrington does not remember meeting Wright before Paris. Also see Michel Fabre, *The Unfinished Quest of Richard Wright*, 2nd edition (Urbana: University of Illinois Press, 1993), 579, which reports on the party from another source.

9. John A. Williams, "My Man Himes: An Interview with Chester Himes," *Amistad 1* (New York: Vintage Books, 1970), 86.

10. Michel Fabre, *The Unfinished Quest of Richard Wright* (New York: William Morrow, 1973), 461–62.

Why I Left America and Other Essays

The Last Days of Richard Wright

The rue Regis is probably the shortest street in Paris. On the left bank, in the Sevres Babylon arrondissement, it is snugly hidden away among antique shops and small art galleries. As with tiny streets the world over, everyone in the rue Regis knows everyone else.

Since the grey and drizzly morning when Monsieur Vallette, the sturdy, reticent *charbonnier* whose tiny bistro and fuel storage cellar occupies one part of No. 4, learned that *'le grande monsieur'* wouldn't be returning home from the clinic, the rue Regis has become one of the most silent streets in Paris. And an urn, containing the ashes of a one time Mississippi black boy more recently one of the greatest writers living in a proud France, has already been deposited in a tiny locker-type bin in Paris' *Cimitier Du Pere Lachaise*.

The great silence in the rue Regis seems almost visually to hover about the closed shutters of a ground floor apartment in No. 4, just the other side of the entrance to Monsieur Vallette's bistro. It is the downthrusting silence of a place where only yesterday there was great activity; great comings and goings.

Occasionally the charbonnier, cloaked in his withdrawn, Auvergnian stolidity, peeks from above the curtains of his bistro as if waiting for someone . . . or perhaps reflecting upon yesterday when there were always cars pulling up to the curb; cars with the CD plates of the embassies or occasionally a minister's car. And of course many ordinary cars and even taxis. There were the visitors, some in ordinary street clothes, others clothed in the chic sophistication which languidly proclaimed Paris *haute couture*; *les etrangers* in their handsome African robes, the American-cut suits, the jaunty fez-type headgear of South Asia, the saris. But now there are only those silent and closed grey shutters and an urn filled with ashes in the Pere Lachaise columbarium.

"*Le grande monsieur*," Richard Wright, won't be coming home ever again.

Inside the entrance to number four, first door to the right just over the doorbell, there is a plain nameplate, M. RICHARD WRIGHT. When that door was in the habit of being opened very, very often, one entered a large, comfortable sitting-room where one was immediately aware of the books, it seemed thousands of books.

The central piece in the large and tastefully cozy room is a huge and deep divan covered in a luxurious emerald green velour. It is difficult not to imagine Dick Wright as he was, seated on the divan with one leg drawn up, arms waving to emphasize a point, holding forth as he loved to do; his phrases filled with laughter, his pronouncements laced with barbs and bitterness. Invariably on the white-tile-topped coffee table in front of the divan there was a pot of steaming coffee or a bottle of Scotch or even a bottle of cognac, though Dick always cautioned you with what his doctor had to say about cognac. "You better watch that stuff," he'd say. "The French just sip cognac but you Americans down it like it was whiskey and first thing you know your heart stops beatin' and then you're really in a fix. Man!" Dick himself only took coffee while he was writing. Scotch or beer, taken sparingly, was allowed for his holidays.

The wall to the right of the divan is broken by two large arched openings without doors. One leads to the old-fashioned bedroom and further on to the white-tiled bathroom, the other to the book-lined study. Above the arches hang two huge beaten brass serving platters presented to Dick as tokens of esteem by a group of Indonesian admirers at Bandung during the historic conference which produced his controversial *Color Curtain*. "Yes," said Dick very often, "when the press asked John Foster Dulles what was goin' on down there in Bandung he just laughed and said they were only havin' a little fish fry. THEM FISH WAS WHALES, BROTHER." Dick's report on that fish-fry was certainly controversial but then all of Dick's books were controversial and he seemed to revel in the storms which followed. He once said to this writer, "They may hate the hell out of what I write but they are forced to read it!" And in his eyes as he said it there was that same barely suppressed glee as one catches in the eye of a schoolboy who has just given someone a hotfoot.

The other side of the living room is almost completely occupied by a tremendous glass-doored bookcase containing copies of Richard Wright in languages ranging from Japanese to Turkish. There are titles in German and Italian and in the Scandinavian languages. *Native Son* in Hebrew, *Black Boy* in Spanish, a huge monument to the sometimes awful struggles of the American Negro to stand on the same level as other men.

In Dick's study as you enter through one of the arched doorways there seems to be a mass of confusion. The practiced eye, however, suddenly realizes that it isn't confusion at all; it is simply a matter of quantity. One side of the room is completely covered with book shelves. They reach from floor to ceiling and there are certainly very few private libraries which can boast of such a vast range of subjects so carefully collected. On the other side of the study there is a manuscript-buried oaken desk-table. A tiny island in the sea of manuscripts is inhabited only by a sturdy Underwood of rather questionable vintage. From this battered, battle-scarred machine poured forth the millions of words; words written in anger and outrage; words of

5

shocking violence, terror and sometimes an echo of ominous laughter. This is the machine which spat out the words which caused critics the world over to use terms like outrageous, insolent, preposterous, naive, magnificent, stupid and brilliant, arrogant and humble. Although Dick loved plunging into battle and gave as well and usually better than he received, still his closest friends knew that too often he was terribly wounded by those among the critics who seemed obsessed with a need to exterminate this upstart from a Mississippi sharecropper's cabin who dared to raise his black voice in protest against their ancient and hallowed institutions. But with the bitterness people occasionally got a fleeting glimpse of another side of the many-sided nature of Dick Wright as they did when, speaking toward the end of November in the American church in Paris he said, "I can find in my heart deep pity for the nigger-hating Georgia cops and those screaming women in front of the New Orleans Schools because the whole experience of slavery and the half slavery which followed destroyed them as men; killed their souls; made them subhuman. After all, you can't burn and castrate the sons of your own fathers and rape the brown daughters who are really your sisters gotten by your fathers on helpless black women without becoming mad, raging animals."

During the past year this was a constantly recurring theme in Wright's conversation. Apparently it had burst into flame when he'd discovered *Mandingo*, a remarkable book based on slave period documents and made into a novel by sociologist Kyle Onstott. Dick Wright was so deeply impressed with this book that he brought it to the attention of the most influential French literary circles. As a result of Wright's efforts the book is now being translated and shall be published in France during the coming spring. "You must read that book to understand what happened to the great American dream" was an often repeated phrase during the last weeks of Wright's life.

The Last Days of Richard Wright

Dick Wright was a man of irrepressible vitality. During a typical afternoon in his Paris apartment one remembers him dashing here and there from his living room "throne" into the study and back again. "Have you seen this?" or "have you heard of that?" His mind seemed constantly running like a terrier sniffing for a still warm rabbit's tracks. He was constantly making plans and, though in his work he was painfully meticulous and his notes and other reference material were tremendously organized, in these plans there seemed to be a complete lack of organization. Certainly there was a zeal but it was the erratic zeal of a mischievous truant. He planned another trip to Africa. He was curious about Cuba and perhaps he'd go there. Then there was China where something of unimaginable magnitude was taking place and he must go there. His hungry mind was already on ten voyages.

Among the various Wright plans was one which amused his friends immensely. Dick wanted to build a circular staircase at one end of his study which would cut through the ceiling to the apartment above. However, although Dick had discussed the staircase with an architect friend who then made his preliminary measurements, the owners of the apartment above hadn't the slightest idea that Dick planned to buy their apartment from them. In fact Dick hadn't even discussed it with them. But his friends knew that Dick was perfectly capable of having that staircase built right up to the ceiling where it would hang until the upstairs tenants "got the message!" One of Dick's friends, Noel Torres, a young Negro international legal expert with the U.N. in Beirut, used to sit staring at the empty space soon to be filled by the staircase. Shaking his head mournfully he'd say, "Dick, why don't you pay me a retainer's fee now because, brother, you're going to need a lawyer come one fine day of ceiling demolishing!" Chester Himes, another old friend, would just stare at Dick with an expression of incredulity mixed with affection and say, "Dick, you're out of your .... mind!"

Although Wright continually spoke of his projected staircase none of his friends realized that it was connected with a carefully guarded secret. The staircase was to be built in Wright's study but undoubtedly, in his mind, the stairway spiralled up to the ceiling, tore through the floor of the House of Commons in London and terminated just in front of the door marked "REGINALD BUTLER . . . British Home Secretary"!

The story was told to this writer less than a year ago in strictest confidence. It may be assumed, however, that under the circumstances the need for secrecy no longer exists . . . and that Dick Wright would be the first to agree to its public exposure.

Some fifteen years ago when Richard Wright and his wife Ellen accepted the invitation of the French government to establish residence in France, Gertrude Stein found an apartment for them in the rue Monsieur Le Prince. It was a huge, rambling old-fashioned apartment in the heart of the *Quartier Latin* surrounded by the ancient buildings of the *Comedie Française*, the *Sorbonne* and the beautiful *Jardins des Luxembourg*.

The Wrights found that there was plenty of room for a growing family and still space to entertain the people who flocked to the Wright home. It is this apartment really, which thousands of visitors associate with the brilliant, much sought after writer. To this apartment came George Padmore who, according to Dick, created Ghana on a London kitchen table. Here also came Jean Paul Sartre and Simone de Beauvoir, Arna Bontemps, Gunnar Myrdal, Dr. E. Franklin Frazier, Claude Barnett, Etta Motten, James Ivy, Frank Yerby, Ralph Ellison, J. Saunders Redding. This was the apartment to which came the great, the not so great, and those who would never be great. All were welcome.

But over the years the excitement of being an *homme celebre* paled and the open house with the menacing, inescapable telephone proved too great a distraction for Wright and he yearned for a hiding place where he could think and write undisturbed. The beautiful old farmhouse which he purchased in 1957 was just that. With a bit of modernization it was made into a comfortable writer's retreat. "A place where I can grow me some potatoes" quipped Wright.

Not far from the sleepy farm village of Ailly, beside a tiny dribble which the chauvinistic Normans proudly called the River Eure, Dick Wright found the peace and quiet he needed. This was probably the happiest period in his life and it was here that he wrote his last great novel *The Long Dream* (just recently published in French and titled *Fishbelly*). It was here, in 1958, that Wright told me that he suddenly realized that above all he was a man of the country. He needed the smoky, dawn-shrouded fields, the ever-busy birds and the cattle lowing in the mist.

Wright actually planted his potatoes, and corn. Later there were peas and beans. There were many writer and artist friends who lived in tiny left bank hotel rooms who didn't know what in the hell to do with the pile of vegetables which Dick dumped proudly on their sloping, linoleum-covered floors where they brewed ferociously strong coffee on tiny alcohol stoves. But Dick was irrepressible and no one had the heart to dampen his enthusiasm with a lecture on the impossibility of balancing a pot filled with corn on a tiny spirit stove.

These were the days of fulfillment for Dick Wright. His family was thriving and happy. Little Rachel, who looks like her mother, was a lovable, mischievous little elf, and Julia, who already bears an almost shocking resemblance to Dick, led all of the students in the French *lycée* system in every subject. In those days Dick seemed to have only one concern and that was with Julia, who worshipped her father and plans a writer's career also. "That child Julia," Dick would say, "she worries me. She won't do anything but study." But his voice never hid the fierce pride. And then one day in 1958 after the final examinations, Julia, not quite 17, received bids from both Oxford and Cambridge Universities.

Wright detested being separated from his family, but it was decided that Julia was too young to go off to England alone. Ellen Wright bundled up children and baggage and purchased a small house in London. Eleven-year-old Rachel entered the French school there (she speaks no English) and Julia prepared to enter Cambridge. Dick, in Paris, was going over the final manuscript for *The Long Dream* and had already started work on a second volume to the novel.

The empty apartment must have seemed too large for Dick alone and he spent more time at Ailly but that didn't seem to fill the void and so, suddenly, without discussing the move with his friends, he sold both the large left bank apartment and the remodelled farmhouse in Normandy and went to join his family in London. He was given the usual three month tourist visa, renewed old English acquaintances and then applied for a permanent residence visa. After much red tape the application of Richard Wright for a residence visa was rejected! Dick and his friends, among them John Strachey, onetime Minister of Defense in the Labour Government, felt that some error had been made by a minor bureaucrat and another application was made. This time there was no room left for doubt. The application was flatly rejected even though it was pointed out that many Americans live in England with residence permits.

Wright was greatly shocked by the unexpected refusal, as was Strachey and a host of influential friends. Telephone calls were made, important names were discreetly dropped where it was hoped some good would come of it. In the end there was a final heated discussion in the Home Office where, according to Wright, a spluttering, red faced official told him that he could expect an extension of 30 days and not one day more and that he'd have to sign a written agreement to this. Wright flatly refused to sign such a statement and in the ensuing argument heated words were exchanged and Wright's passport was thrown to the floor by the official, who then turned and walked away.

A furiously bitter Richard Wright returned to Paris. To this writer he said, "They simply do not want non-white people living in England. They don't want Africans and Jamaicans, but to keep them out they've got to change their laws and endorse the KEEP BRITAIN WHITE crowd, but this might be embarrassing in the Commonwealth!"

That is the story of the stairway in the rue Regis. John Strachey has questioned the Government several times in Parliament in an effort to get a clear statement of policy in this matter and these discussions have been documented in *Hansard*, the British equivalent of our *Congressional Record*.

Mr. Reginald Butler, the British Home Secretary, has several times blithely parried these questions in the Wright affair but Dick had promised Strachey to avoid publicity until he could get a straightforward policy declaration from the Tory Government. In the meantime Dick found the much smaller apartment in the rue Regis and, looking forward to the time when Ellen and the girls returned to Paris for their vacations, hoped to buy the apartment immediately above, "with a winding staircase built into my study so that we won't have to go out into the hall to get up there."

Back in Paris, Wright plunged into his work and into the turbulent, stimulating life which only the French capital offers. None of his friends, with the exception of this writer, knew of the brief, bitter London experience. However, it must be said that Wright continued to believe in the basic honesty and element of fair play of the British people. And, too, it is difficult to retain much bitterness in the rare luminosity which filters through the tiny streets of Paris.

The last two years of his life were a time of prolific output.

11

Dick's working days as always began at 7 a.m. with the sturdy Underwood chattering and banging inexorably until 2 in the afternoon. Then the neighbors would smile a greeting as "Monsieur Reeshard" bounced into the street to rush off to the tiny English Bookshop in the quaint rue de Seine. There would be Mlle. Gaite, a charming Frenchwoman who seems to blossom when surrounded by writing folk. Gaite would brief Dick on the latest literary gossip or haul out a few rare titles she knew he'd want. Later perhaps, Dick's beret-crowned figure could be seen in the rue Tournon on his way to the Cafe Tournon, a literary hangout in the shadow of the huge *Palais du Luxembourg*, which is also the French Senate.

The Tournon was Dick's favorite afternoon cafe in a Paris where everyone has a favorite cafe, and he could always be assured of an argument with his coffee. The catalyst here is Madame Alazard, a darkly handsome Frenchwoman who runs things like a tough but affectionate drill sergeant. She is aware of all of the romances and the scandals, the hopes and blasted hopes. For Dick Wright, Madame Alazard bore an affection bordering on worship.

It would be more than stretching a point if it were assumed that everyone in the Tournon regarded Wright with the same affection. There is also a tight band of Americans who never tried to cloak their outright hatred of the great Negro writer. They would often attack Wright in the most insulting manner, referring to his books and his opinions with contempt. They hurled the term "expatriate" at Wright with a venom which shocked the listening French and other European intellectuals. One young Israeli poet once asked, "But why does such a great and world famous writer sit so patiently and try to answer the insults of these savage people. If Faulkner or Hemingway ever came here they wouldn't even dare ask them questions." Then the young poet quietly concluded, "But of course. It is only because he is a black man and they feel that they have the right to say what they wish to him!"

Actually, this attitude was only a reflection of the attitude of the Paris American community toward Wright. Although there were some friends and admirers like the Reverend Clayton Williams at the American Church of Paris, for the most part Americans viewed Wright with distaste. Wright avoided them as much as possible. His relations with representatives in Paris of the American press too was somewhat less than warm. He was always referred to as "the expatriate Wright." But Wright pointed out that F. Scott Fitzgerald was an expatriate and Hemingway is an expatriate but they are white and a white writer has a right to be whatever he wants, expatriate or ex anything. "But a Negro has to go to the good white folks and ask 'Please, Mister Boss-man, kin I please be an ex somethin', suh?'"

Wright was deeply suspicious of the press and perhaps because of this often played into the hands of a journalist who wanted to take him down a peg. At the time of his death he was considering a suit against a mass circulation news magazine which had quoted him in an article on Negroes in Paris when, as a matter of fact he had refused an interview with their correspondent. Nevertheless, the magazine quoted him in a manner which at least one could say would win no new readers for Richard Wright. To add to the injury the article ended on a high note of praise for a young Negro writer who had just quit France and returned to the U. S.[1]

Perhaps the magazine did not know that the young writer had been deported by the French government when it was found that he had written letters and articles to American and British periodicals over the forged signature of another Negro living in Paris. The actual forger was apprehended by the French *Surette* (FBI) where he signed a long confession. Ironically, he would have been sent to a long prison term if Wright

---

13

and the victim of the forgeries hadn't intervened . . . again to spare the Negro community a messy situation. Wright kept complete police files on this case and had planned using the sordid affair as a theme in his next novel. "Man, I don't have to write novels. I just sit here and let 'em happen. Then the critics say 'Wright has been away from home too long and this sort of thing doesn't happen anymore.'" This was almost one of the last things that Dick Wright ever said.

During the spring and summer months of the past year Wright spent virtually all of his time as the guest of a French family, manufacturers of a soft drink called *Verrigood*. Their estate covers miles of forest covered hills along the River Seine. The estate has become a haven for liberal intellectuals and is called Moulin D'Andade, taking its name from the breathtakingly beautiful and ancient flour mill or *moulin*. Among the guests who thronged to the Moulin D'Andade one always found movie stars, directors, poets, novelists, African diplomats, people from the theatre and an occasional painter. Of them all Monsieur Reeshard was the most sought after. He could always be counted on for the most bizarre, the most excruciatingly funny tales. Dick, or Monsieur Reeshard, had a permanent room in the moulin and it was here that Dr. E. Franklin Frazier and I visited him in July.

When Dick wasn't tramping in the woods or sitting with the voluble Norman peasants in a cafe "down the road," he was engrossed in his newest obsession. One uses the term obsession because Dick admitted that since he'd discovered it he was completely incapable of stopping. A few months earlier he had asked a young South African writer what was the book he was carrying under his arm. It was Dick's introduction to Hai-Kai, a form of ancient Japanese poetry which flourished in Nippon between the fifteenth and seventeenth centuries. Buddhistic in origin these poems never exceed three or four lines with no more than from five to seven words to each line. The Japanese philosophers used them as a form of conversation or *jeu d'esprit* but Wright found in them a remarkable control of words and symbols and plunged into one of his characteristically meticulous and exhaustive studies. At the time of his death Dick had written more than one thousand poems in this form and, as pointed out by his wife Ellen just a few days ago, had subtly changed the quality of the ancient Hai-Kai and had injected a Negro flavor which she felt enriched them tremendously. Poring at random over the poems in the shuttered Wright apartment just a few days ago the writer selected these poems for the EBONY piece, the first ever published of examples of the Hai-Kai poems of Richard Wright.

I am nobody
A red sinking Autumn sun
Took my name away

Make up your mind snail!
You are half inside your house
And halfway out!

In the falling snow
A laughing boy holds out his
*   palms*
Until they are white

Whose town did you leave
O wild and drowning spring
*   rain*
And where do you go?

Keep straight down this block
Then turn right where you will
*   find*
A peach tree blooming

With a twitching nose
A dog reads a telegram
On a wet tree trunk

The spring lingers on
In the scent of a damp log
Rotting in the sun

The crow flew so fast
That he left his lonely caw
Behind in the fields

Although Dick Wright was known among his associates in the writing craft as a prolific producer, his writing and associated activities mounted to an unprecedented intensity during the last six months of his life. There were lectures, interviews, radio and TV broadcasts, which would have very seriously taxed the energies of anyone else. Wright died Monday night, November

28. Friday night, December 2, the Radio Television Française broadcast on their major network the fourth in a series of four planned broadcasts by the celebrated author. In this final broadcast which was titled "Homage to Richard Wright" Madame Hélène Bokanowski, the wife of Michel Bokanowski, Minister of Communications in the De Gaulle cabinet, expressed her sorrow and the sorrow of France over the loss of "one of the greatest American Writers."

There has been a great deal of criticism in Paris' American circles over these broadcasts whose major theme was the problem of racism in America (with some emphasis on the current integration hysteria in New Orleans) and in the rest of the world too. But Wright's position was and has always been in direct opposition to his sensitive critics who condemned his utterances and his writings too as being anti-American. "Absolute hogwash," declared Wright many times. "I know America. I know what a great nation and people America could be but it won't be until there is only *one* American, regardless of his color or his religion or anything else. That's where my critics have to spill their bile. Not on me for daring to tell the truth, but on those real anti-Americans who won't let America become what she can and will be."

Wright's last spurt went into another form of activity, certainly a less tiring one. Through an acquaintance and admirer in the German Embassy in Paris, Wright was encouraged to try his great talents in the field of radio playwriting. Over the past six months several of his radio plays have been aired in Germany with tremendous popular success. Dick Wright once revealed to me that the themes for these plays came directly out of JET magazine. As an example; his latest play was a rather bitter satire on the problems confronting a southern family where the wife shot the maid in the belief that her rather alcoholic husband was having an affair with the Negro woman. As a matter of fact the husband *had* made several passes at the curiously muscular maid who, after the shooting, was discovered to be a man!

One night roughly three months ago Dick Wright took the brilliant young Doctor Schwarzmann, who was treating his intestinal disorder, to dinner at Leroy and Gabby Haynes' in the rue Manuel in the heart of Pigalle. Dick was in the habit of going up to Haynes whenever he could "just to be with the folks," also it must be said, to swap tales with Leroy and Mezz Mezzrow and others whose fame as raconteurs challenged even Dick Wright. And it must be said too that there is no place else in Europe where "the faithful" can find a real barbecued rib or a few feet of chittlin's with a mess of real greens.

Among the gentlefolk avidly working on their fried chicken or ribs was Nicole Barclay, a dynamic and completely unpredictable Frenchwoman who heads Barclay disques. Barclay's is probably the leading French house in jazz recordings and more famous Negro musicians work under a Barclay contract than any other. Although Dick had lived in France for almost fifteen years it was his first meeting with Nicole. He was asked to call her and when he did a luncheon was arranged. Dick left the table a jazz critic. Nicole, with her great charm, had persuaded him to write the reviews on the back covers of the Barclay label jazz discs. When he left his apartment to enter the clinic for that last check-up his work table was covered with manuscripts, essays and the writings of the most astute musicologists in the field of jazz. In the living room there was a formidable pile of records and a stereophonic outfit which Nicole had just sent to him.

In Paris' Eugene Gibez clinic during the night of November 28, death found Dick Wright. He'd gone to the clinic for a physical check-up, as he'd been in the habit of doing every few months since fighting off a case of intestinal amoeba picked up in Africa four years ago. His family was in London and since Dick expected to be in the clinic only two days or so he hadn't bothered to tell anyone that he was going there but he did have his telephone service switch all of his calls there. When this writer called on the 29th, he was told, "Monsieur Wright died during last night!" A nurse in the clinic told me later that he had been gay, filled with his endless stories when she'd left his room that evening. He was to leave the next morning. Fifteen minutes later her night bell sounded and in three minutes when she entered the room again he had already breathed his last. It was a very sudden heart attack, she told me, and he never realized that he was going.

After the funeral for a very few friends in the columbarium at the Pere Lachaise cemetery, Ellen Wright and Julia solemnly returned to the Rue Regis to close their shutters and to mourn their dead. A few days later when I visited them they had recovered from the shock and could discuss their plans. Dick's death had changed everything. Julia has given up Cambridge; she'll return to attend the Sorbonne because that is what Dick had always wanted. Most of all she wants to see America. "I want to visit Daddy's home in Mississippi," she told me. Later she would like to teach for a while at a place like Fisk University. But most of all she wants to write "like daddy."

Ellen Wright plans to devote her life to Dick's work, the finished and the unfinished. There was a play, *Daddy Goodness*, which must be produced. There are those Hai-Kai poems to be published. She'll begin all of this after little Rachel has been brought back to her French lycée. Taking me by the arm she took me into Dick's study. "I found this on the wall," she said. And tacked to the wall was a great sheaf of notes, some typewritten, others in pencil. Dick had started to take an inventory of his work. There on the wall was listed everything he'd ever written: articles, essays, short stories, their dates, where they'd been published. Everything would have been there in a few more days. "It's as if he was telling me what he wanted me to do," said Ellen Wright.

The Last Days of Richard Wright

NOTE

1. Harrington is referring to "Amid the Alien Corn," *Time*, 72 (November 17, 1958), 28, where the following appears about Wright:

> Richard (*Native Son*) Wright, the dean of Negro writers abroad, says bluntly, "I like to live in France because it is a free country. Then there are my daughters. They are receiving an excellent education in France." What of the danger of getting out of touch with U. S. life? Snaps Wright, "The Negro problem in America has not changed in 300 years."

The "young Negro writer" mentioned by Harrington was Richard Gibson, who forged an inflammatory letter over Harrington's signature.

The Mysterious Death of
Richard Wright

In the Impressionist atmosphere of a tiny Paris sidewalk cafe on the Boulevard St. Germain Des Pres one afternoon during the 1950s, Richard Wright ruminated aloud, "Art is such a ruthless taskmaster that when the artist stumbles perhaps he pays with his life." Long after that afternoon I realized that with this enigmatic statement he was offering me his complete trust. It was as if he'd opened a tiny window behind which lurked an enormous secret agony . . . and perhaps a foreboding knowledge too.

Wright had slaved under the taskmaster. He was already the celebrated author of a remarkable book of short stories, *Uncle Tom's Children*; an autobiography which had become a monumental classic and reference book to a generation of sociologists, *Black Boy*; a prophetic novel, *Native Son*, which had been translated into most languages; and a perceptive novel in two volumes, *The Long Dream*, the second volume of which, oddly, has never been published. This oddity has been made even more intriguing by the recent publication of a manuscript called *American Hunger*, which the publishers tell us is a "discovery." Well, perhaps it is a discovery and then again perhaps it isn't.

Talking with Wright in those days about art and life it was

impossible to visualize him only a few years earlier as a scrawny Black kid, numbly fighting to exist in the concentration camp-plantation system of Mississippi. In little more than 10 years he'd 'escaped' to Chicago, taught himself to read and write at night while washing dishes and running errands during the day, and finding himself dazed and shaking alongside Edgar Allan Poe, Jack London, Ambrose Bierce and Ernest Hemingway. I can't recall anything to match this in any literature.

Wright was an American phenomenon. Lenin, during the Russian Revolution, looked at the jubilant former serfs who'd changed the course of history. Wouldn't he be thinking also of one like this one when he dreamed of creating a new man? Phenomena—especially Black ones—can't be measured by ordinary standards. Perhaps this is what W. E. B. DuBois had in mind when he said, "We struggle not only for the right of Blacks to be right but also for their right to be wrong!"

Wright was a prodigious reader and he never failed to credit the extraordinary 10-year leap from semi-illiterate Black serf to literary giant to his discovery of Marx, Engels and Lenin, which subsequently led to his membership in the Communist Party. Mississippi had taught him to despise capitalist exploitation and injustice. The Party showed him how to channel that hatred.

But never once in the 10 years I knew him in Paris did he ever speak of the circumstances surrounding his leaving the Party or of his contributing an essay to a book by six ex-Communists called *The God That Failed*, which became sort of a bible of the Cold War. His obvious avoiding of this period was so uncharacteristic of the man that it pointed to the source of his secret, almost unbearable agony. I can only imagine that it was the case of an extraordinarily talented youth reaching for the sky being allowed to climb into the cockpit of a sophisticated supersonic jet plane and taking off, on his first try.

These recollections were intensified the other day when I received a copy of *American Hunger*. Reading what the publishers had to say on the dustjacket and the accompanying essay by Sorbonne professor Michel Fabre I was not convinced that anyone really thought it was a 'discovery.' If I were asked to describe what I thought it was I would consider the term mugging to be more applicable because publication of this manuscript amounts to the mugging of a dead genius!

I remembered an evening in the panelled bar of a small hotel near UNESCO where Dick, Chester Himes and I had joined E. Franklin Frazier, who was frequently in Paris as a UNESCO expert on sociology. We were talking about the organized crippling of Black kids by the very schools which were supposed to be educating them. Naturally, I suppose, we found ourselves discussing Dick's *Black Boy*.

It was then I learned that when he'd finished the manuscript and thought about it for a while—which must have been some time after he left the Communist Party—Wright had resolutely eliminated the final section of the book because it obviously detracted from its anti-racist, anti-fascist message. He'd never permit that manuscript to be published, he exclaimed with his usual vehemence. I had the impression that he'd destroyed the manuscript. Apparently that was a false assumption because now, 16 years later, it has been published as *American Hunger*!

The question is: Why was *American Hunger* published 16 years after the death of this great anti-fascist, anti-racist Black master, against his wishes? The reason seems to me at least to be clumsily obvious. Americans, no matter what their color or ethnic roots, have been viciously savaged and betrayed by a system which has throttled the decency and democracy which is at the real root of the nation. Anything is permitted in the race for profit. The result is an unprecedented amount of economic hardship, unbelievable corruption and cynicism.

Only in those parts of the world which have embraced socialism has this state of affairs been eliminated, and that fact is being recognized more and more—even in the United States. This represents a real danger to a broken-down system. The discredited establishment answers with the old mouldy anti-communism.

American Hunger, written in a burst of frustration and be-wilderment by a young Black genius, can be placed in that category, although the dead author was anything but anti-Communist. But to a system attempting to crawl off the fly-paper of Watergate, where 115 members of Congress are on the payroll of a fascist dictator, and where the KKK helps patrol the Mexican border, what is one more betrayal?

One morning in 1956, Dick Wright telephoned me to lunch at his flat in the Rue Regis. Over lunch I realized that he was in quite an emotional state. Never much of a drinker, he seemed to be outdoing himself on the Bordeaux. After a while he looked up. "Ollie," he said, "you know about *The God That Failed*." Yes, I replied, I knew about it. There was an expression of anguish on his face as he told me that a 10th anniversary edition was to be published. Richard Crossman, the British Labor MP had called him the night before with the suggestion that he should write a new essay for the planned edition. (Incidentally, Cross-man had been one of the six writers in the original edition.) Wright refused—rather furiously I gathered—and told Cross-man to tell them—and he emphasized the word "them"—that he would write an essay on racism and the cloak and dagger terrorism which was poisoning the climate around the expatri-ate Paris community. "They can publish that in their god-damned 10th anniversary issue."

Suddenly he began to laugh uproariously. "Do you know why the cafes in the Quarter are crowded up 'till the last minute," he asked. "Well," he answered himself, "it's because all those CIA informers can't leave until the one customer who ain't an agent leaves with the lady agent he thinks he picked up." Peals of laughter—and I knew that he'd just shut his little window again.

From that time Wright seemed obsessed with the idea that the FBI and the CIA were running amuck in Paris. He was thoroughly convinced that Blacks were special targets of their cloak and dagger activities and that several of his African friends with leadership possibilities were being eliminated, citing especially the case of the African surgeon with whom he'd met only a week before the man collapsed in Geneva. In the hospital to which he'd been taken he told doctors he was convinced that he'd been poisoned. He'd diagnosed the symptoms, identified the probable poison and prescribed the necessary treatment. Incredibly, he was treated for an ordinary stomach disorder and died in a few agonizing hours.

At about the same time, Wright became co-organizer and chairman of a Franco-American group of artists and intellectuals in a movement to free Communist Party leader Henry Winston from federal prison and planned to tour Europe in that role. For him it was a period of feverish activity; a period in which Richard Wright, the mature man, was trying to square accounts with Richard Wright the mature artist.

Most of his acquaintances were appalled over his lack of caution. But if they'd been asked what there was to be cautious about they would have been unable or unwilling to answer.

For this, however, they must be forgiven for it was long before a thoroughly frightened world press exposed the chilling record of blackmail, extortion, robbery, unexplained disappearances and torture, murders carried out by the secret armies of the FBI and the CIA. Paris, particularly in its centuries-old center of intellectual activity, the Latin Quarter, seemed to have been selected as a vital target by these "patriotic" criminals.

Of all the many Americans living in France, Dick Wright was the only one who was publicly saying these things then! One of his most effective efforts was an expose for the French radio in five parts which were broadcast weekly. The fifth and last part was broadcast one week after his death from what was diagnosed as a heart attack!

Among the many lovable contradictions in the personality of this very complex artist was his laughingly admitted hypochondria. It was a source of great fun and ribbing between Chester Himes, Dick and me, with Chester chidingly reminding him that he was one of the most vitally alive brimming-over-with-health cats in the world. Dick's jovial answer was "Yeah. But man, one never knows, does one?"

Once every six months Dick drove out to Neully's American Hospital for a thorough weekend checkup, pointing out that if, for example, anyone was interested in doing you in, they'd never dare it in the American Hospital. But he always called either Chester or me to let us know exactly when he was going in. We viewed it as a minor eccentricity.

One wintry weekend in 1961 I visited friends in Normandy. On Monday morning I returned to Paris where the concierge handed me a telegram which had arrived the night before. It was from Dick and simply said, "OLLIE PLEASE COME TO SEE ME SOON AS YOU GET THIS." It gave the name and location of a clinic I'd never heard of. Mystified, I phoned the clinic and asked to speak with Monsieur Richard Wright. I was told that it would not be possible. "Monsieur Wright died last night!"

After the first shock I managed to stammer a request to see him and was told that there seemed to be no reason why not. I immediately rushed to the clinic, at the seedier end of the Rue Vaugirard, where I was permitted to see the body and was told that he'd been admitted for a checkup on Saturday morning.

Sunday afternoon at about five, I was told, he rang for his nurse. When she arrived she found that he was dead. It was the first time in more than 10 years that he'd not gone to the American Hospital. And it was the only time he'd failed to call either me or Chester Himes!

How Bootsie Was Born

As I remember it the year was 1936, a bad year in most every-body's book.[1] Ellis the cabdriver used to say that even the grays downtown were having it rough but I don't know about that because I lived in Harlem and stayed in Harlem like most members. Anyway, there were a terrible lot of us brethren squeezed in between Central Park, which was as far south as most of us were willing to let our thoughts dwell, and the 155th Street bridge across the Harlem River to the north. To the west it was St. Nicholas Avenue and Park Avenue to the east. That was Harlem and that was where Brother Bootsie was born.

I remember that it was 1936, because it was the year of the Berlin Olympics and Obie McCollum, the chief editor of the *New York Amsterdam News*, had one of his rare bad days and sent his star, all-round newshawk to cover the event. Since one of the duties of the Berlin-bound member had been providing the "Dam" News with cartoons, his departure left a hole in the staff which I was supposed to plug up temporarily. Luckily, not much imagination was needed for the job. I simply recorded the almost unbelievable but hilarious chaos around me and came up with a character. It seems that one of the local numbers runners dug my cartoon and as you probably know, no-body covers as much Harlem territory as the numbers man. And so the cartoon's popularity grew by word of *his* mouth . . .

"Here Brother Bootsie, take this extra hammer I got here in case
the gentlemens of the law decides that this demonstration
is *too* peaceful!"

which was *very* big. About the same time an enterprising root man got into the act.

Now as any P.S. 139 schoolboy could have told you, the root man's job isn't nearly finished when he sells you a bag of old stones and some High John the Conqueror to provide you with staying power. After all, what good is technology in the boudoir without money in your pockets? So the root man also sold you a dream book and several possible hits. Advertising this fantastic offer he began pasting copies of my humble cartoon in his little shop window with the previous day's number written across the top. Well, between the numbers cat, the root man and the rising circulation, I was a made man. McCollum jumped my salary from seven dollars a week to ten and I was able to resign from Father Divine's famous eatery in 135th Street where you could knock yourself out for two bits and a fervent avowal of "Wonderful Peace." I immediately transferred my chowing activities to Rosalie's, a basement hash joint next door to the newspaper which boasted a more socially select herd of feeding members. The rarified social atmosphere of this eatery was due to a combination of circumstances . . . part pigs' tails and collard greens, part hot rolls and deep dish peach cobbler and that part of the clientele which sneaked down off Sugar Hill to partake of these gastronomic delights, lured no doubt by Rosalie's congenital inability to say "no" to any proposition. Incidentally, the cat who was sent to cover the Olympics in Berlin never made it. A post-mortem on the case revealed that he'd gotten hung up in a Paris juice joint. But our man was cool. He sent back about twenty postcard-sized photos showing a bird's eye view of the stadium and all 100,000 spectators. On the back of each photo, which reeked of Guerlain's Parfum, he had written captions with what appeared to be a Max Factor eyebrow pencil. The captions read: "Jesse Owens winning the 100 meters" . . . "The great finish of the 200 meter sprints with U.S. Jesse Owens in first place!"

How Bootsie Was Born

Now I ask you, how could a cartoonist miss? There I was right in the middle of all of this action. I didn't have to think up gags. All I had to do was walk across to The Big Apple, or Small's, latch on to a shorty and watch. The cartoons drew themselves. After a while a jolly, rather well fed but soulful character emerged and crept into each drawing. Ted Poston, the world's loudest and fastest-talking journalist, who was city editor on the *Amsterdam*, named the character Bootsie and Bootsie it has been ever since. And I was more surprised than anyone when Brother Bootsie became a Harlem household celebrity, not only among the colored proletariat but among the literati as well. It could be dangerous though. Like what happened one Saturday morning.

Some unschooled, contemporary cats may believe that the center of the universe during the "hungry thirties" was the Savoy Ballroom but nothing could be farther from the truth. The real center was the Elite Barber Shop, old man Garrison's wire clipping emporium on Seventh Avenue just a few doors above 135th Street. Although by modern standards it would go down as a small joint (there were only five chairs and two raised shoe shine stands) every known Home of the period was shorn or fried regularly on these premises. Each Saturday morning some of America's top second class citizens filled the Elite air with spirited public debate on such varied subjects as women, horses, politics, show business, surgery (both amateur and professional) and on what the s.o.b.'s were doing to keep the colored man down. The famous heads which demanded the tonsorial attentions of Pop Garrison and Co. included such notables as Bojangles, Joe Louis, The Black Eagle, Judge Hubert Delaney, Dr. Louis Wright, the Mills Brothers, Walter White, Lester Granger, "Pig Meat" Markham, and Broadway Rose. When Joe Louis was in the chair, traffic was tied up on both sides of Seventh Avenue and to get into the Elite that day you had to have a B.A., a B.S. (which didn't always mean Bachelor of

Science), an M.D., Ph.D., or D.T.'s. But let me tell you about *that* Saturday morning.

I had just liquidated a real crazy *poisson meunierre a la rein* . . . or, fried fish and rice (Rosalie had visited France once) at Rosalie's counter and I felt like digging some way-out tales and light signifying, and so, when I left the eatery I headed for the Elite. Just as I reached the entrance there was a flash and and whoosh . . . man, just like the launching pad at Cape Canaveral! A cat shot out of the door, face covered with lather and new fried hair flying in the breeze. Behind him, waving a razor with an air of dedicated concentration, sprinted Brother Walker, one of the venerable barbers. Alas, the track was too fast and Brother Walker lost his quarry around about 138th Street when his poor old barber's feet cut out on him. But the fleet-footed client had to take his head elsewhere for future conking and general beautifying. Dismukes, my barber, explained that it was all about a tactless remark the missing member had made to the effect that Brother Walker reminded him of the cartoon character, Mister Bootsie . . . and didn't he pose for the cartoonist? The joint was in a merry uproar for hours after and each new batch of clients got a complete rundown on the action from Mister Chappie, the shoeshine "boy." Brother Walker maintained a dignified but hurt silence while I tried to play it cool although I was newly awakened to the dangers of having created a popular Harlem cartoon. But Brother Bootsie thrived on it!

To really dig Brother Bootsie, his trials and tribulations, you'd have to see Harlem from the sidewalk. Everyone in Harlem had trials and tribulations because everyone in Harlem was colored. Or almost everyone . . . John Hammond, Archer Winston and the Baron Timmie Rozencrantz were not colored and yet they were devoted Harlemites. But being colored, even in an enlightened northern burg like New York, could be a drag. Of course there were a few restaurants downtown where the grays wouldn't panic if a member appeared and ordered a meal. But it would take a strong constitution to pass off the ground glass and other delicate spices they were apt to drop into that particular serving. And so most members stayed and laughed and cried in Harlem. There was *some* integration, however.

Practically all of the gentlemen of the police were Paddys. Hoods like Dutch Schultz, Owney Madden and Boo Boo Hoff came to Harlem nightly . . . and departed in the morning with the loot. All on the up and up though, because they owned practically all of the lucrative real estate like Connie's Inn and the Cotton Club. Thousands of other ofays came up nightly to "study the Negro." At times these study groups became so enthralled in their scholarly pursuits that the vice squads had broken down the doors and pulled back the blankets before they realized that their research was about to be tampered with. One of the world's most publicized aristocrats who later became a king (though he would have much preferred being made queen), danced nightly in a fruity joint called *Chez Clinton*. A girl child named Billie Holiday poured out her broken heart at the Elk's Rendezvous while a young laundry girl named Ella made new, unheard-of sound with Chic Webb at the Savoy. The Black Eagle took off on the first nonstop flight to Africa and landed out of gas twenty-eight miles away in the Flushing mud flats, while there were persistent rumors that Father Divine would step from another airplane onto a cloud to show Harlemites the true road.

Downtown the psychoanalyst's couch joined the casting couch as style Americana and the grays beat their shallow breasts and sobbed, "Where, oh where, Lord, did we goof?" It was the time of the great guilt and they flocked to the Roxy and the Palace to watch evil Indians sink feathered arrows into the good guys, who kicked a couple of times and then split the scene. The sobs and groans of the audiences were heard deep underground where the "A" Train sped home to Harlem. And the same flicker would hit the Alhambra and the Regent a couple of months later but here, when the long-suffering pioneers collected red arrows and bullets in their pale frames, the colored folks rolled in the aisles, laughin' and laughin'. And Brother Bootsie was right in there laughin' and gigglin' too . . . but he could never figure out why. And one night in the Harlem Moon over a few gins with gingerales Langston Hughes told Bootsie it was very simple. He was just laughin' to keep from cryin'. And out front at the bar, Yarborough, the Bishop's chauffeur, yelled, "Bartender. Give the professor another shorty of gin there."

A little scoople-headed runt walked along 117th Street munching on a bag of day-old buns. As I passed him he stopped working his little jaws and said, "Hey Mithter, you know one thing? White folks shore is dumb. Why? Well, I'll tell ya why. Now take this Mithter Kelley . . . he's my white teacher over at the school. And I'm settin' there in my seat in the las' row, an' he says, 'Leroy' . . . tha's me. 'Leroy is you asleep?' Man, I didn't say nothin'. I jest set there lookin' at him. So he says, 'Leroy, is you asleep?' An' I kept settin' there lookin' at him. An' then I says . . . yeah! yeah! yeah!"

Another rat chewed up another colored infant over in one of the Fifth Avenue slums and a downtown tabloid editorialized that perhaps something ought to be done because so many rats were eating up so many Harlem babies, and the rats might become so well fed and bad enough to move downtown and start chewing on the grays! But alack and alas . . . real estate operators in other parts of the city couldn't be expected to go along with letting the coloreds break out of Harlem into their nice real estate, because the "values would drop." So New York's mayor started reading the comics over the radio every Sunday morning!

Ras something or other put on a turban and a black uniform and, perched up on a ladder in 125th Street in front of Herbert's

Diamonds, hipped the crowd on the virtues of the color black. *Buy black, act black, be black.* As a matter of fact, screamed the good Ras, all the great cats in history were black, from Julius Caesar to Beethoven, President Harding, Mickey Mouse and even Santa Claus. His listeners filled the streets and for the first time Harlem saw paddy cops tip-toeing.

The Snakeman, who naturally enough was called Snakes, roamed Harlem teasing giggling women and children with his wooden snakes and alligators and occasionally selling one. And all the time he was laughin' and laughin'. Every member loved old Snakes and every schoolchild knew that he'd once been caught in a Texas mob which was joyously barbecuing another Negro. And when old Snakes started laughing the pecks stared in amazement and let him walk right through. He never stopped walking until he reached the Big Apple . . . and he ain't stopped laughing yet.

The Black Eagle sent a telegram to Hermann Goering, Hitler's Luftwaffe marshal. It was a challenge to an air duel at 40,000 feet above the English Channel. Brother Bootsie happens to know that it was all done with the aid of a bottle of Haig and Haig. That irrepressible rascal, Ted Poston, then with the *Pittsburgh Courier*, just happened to need a story that night, just happened to have the pinch-bottle, and just happened to run into the Eagle. A little light signifying and Goering was a challenged cat. It could have been a coincidence, but Poston beat the metropolitan dailies with his story and the record will show that the *Courier* paid for the Haig and Haig and the telegram. But Max Schmeling punched the Brown Bomber into blissful slumber and all of the pimps had to sell their golf clubs and move down off the Hill. Ellis, the taxi driver, was overheard to say that this was going to be a night for the three efs, which I gathered meant the Fightin', Love-makin' and Footracin'.

But Harlem was flexing her muscles and had eyes for Washington Heights. Ben Davis was elected to the New York City

Council and Paul Robeson sang to an election rally in front of the Theresa Hotel. The grays downtown were in a state of panic. When the mounted cops moved in to break up a torchlight parade outside the Theresa Hotel the stuff hit the fan. The tactics used by these Cossacks were usually successful since it involved backing their horses' behinds into colored faces and hollering "back up." But since this was a torchlight parade, well, the brothers were quite naturally carrying magnesium torches held straight out in front of them like Little David's sword. And so, glossy horse behinds backed right into magnesium torches and Harlem was suddenly witnessing its own Kentucky Derby. Many of the blue uniformed jockeys were left at the post but the hustlers were placing bets on a fast field heading for the Central Park lake. Brother Bootsie shook his head and chuckled . . . or maybe it was me who shook his head and chuckled. Anyway, by that time I didn't know who was Bootsie and who was me!

NOTE

1. Actually, Harrington has confused the chronology slightly. He began to contribute his single panel cartoon *Dark Laughter* to the New York *Amsterdam News* on 25 May 1935. The first appearance of a character named Bootsie was in the panel for 28 December 1935. Bootsie would appear in nearly every *Dark Laughter* cartoon thereafter in the *Amsterdam News*.

Our Beloved Pauli

The Bronx street where I grew up must have been the world's puniest black ghetto, one block long, and only half of it at that. On the other side of the street were the pungent Sheffield Farms stables whose sleek tenants in their warm stalls were the envy of every shivering black kid on the block. Our hopes were aimed low: a chunk of cardboard to plug the holes in our shoe soles, a bit of fat meat swimming in gravy and on Sunday, if God's mood was up to it, chicken. Our dreams, or at least my dreams, were more daring. Visions of Miss Murray[1] made into fine hash by the wheels of a locomotive, in slow motion and color. She was the teacher who lasciviously licked her thin lips each time she told our class that all black kids belonged in the trash baskets. How our little white classmates giggled under the psychedelic kick of these first trips on racism. Another joyous dream, awake or asleep, was the howling death of Duffy, that blue-uniformed menace who lurked in the alley next to Belsky's candy store, hungry nightstick twirling on leather thong. Duffy's stick had already put Melvin Toles into bed. He was only nine, but paralysis would keep him there for life. We didn't realize it then, probably because the jack-leg preacher over at Thessalonia Baptist had explained that Melvin was only "kind'a sprained by the Law." Each Fourth of July Duffy's fat buttocks pranced along the Grand Concourse in the Veterans of

"Doctor Jenkins, before you read us your paper on inter-stellar gravitational tensions in thermo-nuclear propulsion, would you sing us a good old spiritual?"

Foreign Wars parade. Duffy always carried the Stars and Stripes.

Mornings, dry or wet, a tiny flock of black mothers stumbled in arthritic disorder over to Grant Avenue where they numbly waited for the penny-pinching white ladies who would hire them for 10 hours. The men folk trudged across the New York Central tracks to Schrimer's umbrella factory or to the ice-plant. Shamefaced they underbid each other for a day's work. The surplus floated back to some day-long card game or sat in squalid flats staring out of the vapor-glazed window panes.

Saturday nights the air seemed to vibrate. "Sportin' folks" clamored into the inevitable rent party where they stomped and rubbed bellies before settin' down to a heap of heavily tabascoed chitlins washed down with tub-fresh gin. Kids along the block lay awake waiting for the explosion of shouting, cussing, screaming and shattering glass. Often after these happenings Reverend Passley, the barber-bricklayer-undertaker (and, some said, root man) had work to do in the part-time mortuary behind the barbershop. The good Reverend had only one oration which began with: "We so confused and upset all the time that we got to lash out at one another. . . ." Unfortunately the folks often lashed out with a straight razor and this inhibited the Reverend's talents considerably. Which is probably why, it was widely whispered, he preferred the ice-pick which left the deceased looking more natural.

Our sources of inspiration were meager. There was Ray Mitchel the "genius" who could "put just about anything together and make a radio out of it." But to be that "deep" called for schooling and such "fool notions" were throttled at birth by the high-minded dedication of Duffy and Miss Murray. One other possible goal was fuzzily sketched by Mr. Sweet Reuban, who not only owned the corner pool-room but also a most formidable pile of gold on constant display in the open showcase of his upper and lower gums. Sweet Reuban would tip back his pearl-

grey, exposing a magnificent head of conked locks and pro-
nounce, "You little 'niggers' will never git nowhere workin' wif
your hands and sweatin' all over the damn place. You ever
heard of a president sweatin'?" With that he would reach into
his vest pocket for the famous gold toothpick and gently dig
around the nuggets with little sucking noises. But by then the
predatory eyes of the oracle were focused on some other world
and we knew that we'd been dismissed.

The kids disappeared one by one into the fog of other black
slums. All except Biffo, our beloved jester. Biffo found his gold-
en hoard—all $17.50 of it—in a night-shuttered tailor shop.
The widowed Polish woman who owned the shop lay in a pool
of her own blood the next morning. Biffo's gravelly laugh
floated up from the dark cellars and vestibules along the block
for several nights. In these hastily commandeered love bowers
Biffo squandered his fortune, converted into chocolate-covered
nut bars, on giggling, squealing teenage girls. Duffy followed
the candied spoor and pounced, delivering Biffo to the plain-
clothes men and eventually the electric chair at Sing Sing. We
climbed the rickety tenement stairs to the flat of Biffo's work-
gnarled father, drawn by whispered rumors of horrible burns
on Biffo's skull. But he lay in a sealed coffin and we quietly
crept out, leaving the huge black father rocking wordlessly over
an oilcloth-covered kitchen table.

My hopeless world was smashed by Meyer Fischer. Every
morning at five Meyer and his wife Blanche rolled in the heavy
ten-gallon milk containers, then tugged and swivelled the
bulky bread baskets to open their unheated grocery store. They
were, and always would be poor Jews because they couldn't
resist mumbled pleas for credit which was rarely repaid. Many
afternoons I sat on a meal sack while Meyer, clasping and un-
clasping his blue-veined hands, his tiny mouth puffing vapor in
the freezing cold store, told me of black poets, teachers, black
doctors. One day he told me of an unbelievable black man

named Paul Robeson. He told me of this black man who was not as good as white men. He had to be, and he was, ten times better. Meyer's piercing eyes refused to release my unbelieving stare. They willed me to think that perhaps there was such a black man! And if there was it would mean that we were not trash and dirt—even though black. It was a soul-splitting thought. It was a blow-torch burning out the foundations of existence. I, along with every child and adult on the block was cruelly maimed by everything I'd ever seen, or heard, or even tasted. We knew that we were a tiny lepers' island surrounded by the "land of the free and the home of the brave." Even the church steeple "crosstown" had its backside turned in our faces. The red-faced butcher, who could barely speak English, kept a special pile of offal for his "nigger trade." If there were ever a Nobel Prize for the vivisection of living, breathing black kids Miss Murray should have had it. Duffy the Law was tearing out palpitating black hearts long before Dr. Barnard left the diaper stage. And when we thought of Duffy we thought of the Stars and Stripes. We were "niggers" and we'd been so magnificently brainwashed in what that meant that the only art, the only poetry in our little "nigger" hearts was:

A chicken aint nothin' but a bird
A nigger aint nothin' but a turd.

The caterpillar, covered with grey-green, undulating hairs, hides its slimy ugliness inside a cocoon. When the season arrives some magic in nature opens the prison and a completely new creature emerges to rest on a leaf in God's air. Gently it folds and unfolds its breathlessly beautiful wings in the strength-building sunlight. Black children carrying their "niggerness" like lead weights on anxiety-tensed shoulders can experience this same metamorphosis. It's happening all around us. On my single-street ghetto it happened when Meyer Fischer first told me of Paul Robeson.

Five years later my "wings" had lifted me out of the tiny Bronx ghetto and set me down in a real people-sized one—Harlem. The rest of America was being cruelly ravaged by the depression but Harlem only giggled over the sounds of self-pity which the wind carried from across the Central Park lake. "Baby, if you crave to see some real, honest-to-goodness depression, come to Harlem, the Home of Happy Feet," giggled the wits on "the turf." I discovered that I wasn't any more hungry learning to draw and paint at the National Academy of Design than I would be huddled up in my room. Anyway it was free and the Academy rooms were warm. At night bunches of us milled around the sidewalk outside the IdleWyle or the Big Apple. Downtown they were still mournfully talking about the good, solid white folks who had walked into space from Wall Street's many windows. Uptown we were talking about Paul Robeson, who was singing songs which gripped some inner fibres in us that had been dozing. And he was saying things which widened black eyes and sharpened black ears, things which sounded elusively familiar. But there were a few cats in the crowd who somehow managed to own one Brooks Brothers suit. They sported frat pins (jimcrow frats) and pretended to read the financial section of *The New York Times* which they'd found on the floor of some Lenox Ave. IRT local. "That damn Robeson," they grumbled, "gon' make the big white folks mad, you just wait and see." They were right. Robeson did make the big white folks mad. But when his voice boomed, I HEAR AMERICA SINGING, he blew flame in the souls of black folk, and a hell of a lot of white folks too, where dim embers had barely glowed since the days of reconstruction.

One blustery night the space between the bar and the lunch counter at the "Harlem Moon" rocked and reeled in the heat of another "Robeson debate." Hopeless fear, cynicism and outraged frustration quickly drew the lines between "Uncle Tom niggers" and "goddamn red niggers." A flat-footed, sad-eyed waiter from New Haven said to me, "Son, them students up there got so much money they don't know what to do. They requires an awful lot of service. Now if you can get together enough for one semester you can hustle your way through." It was a long story but I got there. One of the waiters in the Chi Psi house where I was installed as head—and only—dishwasher asked me, "How in the hell did a little-assed 'nigger' like you get to come to Yale?" All I could answer was, "I guess it was Paul Robeson." "What," he gasped, "you know Paul Robeson?" I lifted a tray of steaming glasses out of the suds and said, "Nope. Just know of him."

My first real job was as art editor of the *People's Voice*. Adam Powell, Charlie Buchanan and Ben Davis published that great sheet and one day Adam called me into his office. "Ollie," he said, "there's someone I want you to meet." A beaming giant of a man left his chair, thumped me on the back with a hand as powerful as John Henry's sledgehammer and boomed, "Feller, I just wanted you to know that those cartoons of yours are great." Of course it was Paul Robeson. I can't remember doing much more than gulping. What can one say to a mountain? But it was the beginning of a treasured friendship.

Paul walked into that ramshackle Harlem newspaper office one afternoon with Ilya Ehrenburg, one of the world's great writers. With them came a tiny slip of a woman, the captain of a Soviet ship which had been torpedoed and sunk in a convoy. Robeson spoke to the staff. Ehrenburg spoke and thanked all Americans, in the name of the Soviet Union, for the weapons the Red Army was putting to such good use against Hitler's killer hordes. And he made it clear that this deep gratitude included all of the people of Harlem. The little ship's captain—I believe her name was Valentina—spoke no English but she beamed as if she'd lived in Harlem all of her life. Later we discovered that she'd lost all of her clothing at sea. In two days a bespectacled black tailor in 126th Street had made her a uniform and overcoat that must have been the pride of the Soviet merchant fleet, MADE IN HARLEM and joyfully paid for by everyone on the staff, from editor to telephone receptionist.

There are many other treasured snapshots engraved in my mind. Paul, a great one for a session of "talkin' and signifyin'," sitting astride an ancient looking desk in the miniature-sized office of his publication *Freedom*. Again I was contributing cartoonist and fascinated spectator. Paul was holding forth on the wizardry of old Josh Gibson, Satchel Paige and other black ballplayers jimcrowed out of what was euphemistically called the national pastime. Listening were editors Lou Burnham and George Murphy, with Lou exploding every now and then with a characteristic, "Amen, Amen!" Behind the desk sat a diminutive secretary whose lovely brown face was illuminated with a serenity which seemed curiously out of place in a loft on 125th Street. "One day," said Paul, "our boys are going to bust right into the Yankee Stadium dugout and teach 'em the fine points of the game." The little secretary's eyes twinkled and she asked, "Mister Robeson, shall I make a note to get a committee together this afternoon?" Paul stopped in mid-sentence and then "fell out." Lou dissolved into a laughter-shaken mass on a pile of newspapers, and George, always cool, sat shaking his head. The secretary who was there gently growing her wings was Lorraine Hansberry.

There are many other memories. A huge sea of black folk silently filling Seventh Avenue as far as one could see. It was Ben Davis' last campaign for a seat on the City Council and it was night, drizzling. Ben had lost, with the help of the cops who somehow managed an epidemic of polling booth breakdowns that day. But the crowds waited patiently outside Ben's election headquarters in the Theresa Hotel. One of the those thoroughly reliable Harlem rumors had it that Paul would sing. "Naw," said someone, "his man lost so what he gon' sing for?" An old church sister just smiled and said, "'Çause he said he would." And then there was Robeson and the heart-filling voice singing WHAT IS AMERICA TO ME.

Not very long ago I was invited by the satirical *Krokodile* to see the Soviet Union. In Tashkent I sat on a parkbench where I could drink in the breathtaking oriental beauty of the opera house. I was thinking of coming back the next day with my sketch pad when a little Uzbek girl came to me holding out a flower. Her oval face was so lovely, even with the tooth missing from in front. Of course I couldn't understand what she was saying but Yuri, my interpreter explained, "She asks if you are Paul Robeson?" Her mother appeared and suddenly it seemed there were hundreds of Uzbek children with their mothers, all carrying hastily picked flowers. I was terribly flustered but I managed to explain that I wasn't Paul Robeson but that he was my friend. And then one Uzbek mother, proud of her English said, "Here, he is our beloved Pauli."

NOTE

1. In "Why I Left America" (see below), this teacher is identified as a Miss McCoy.

Look Homeward Baby

Back in the late 1930's, Small's Paradise may have been some-what less than heavenly. It did, however, boast of a bartender who sent spirits soaring and the proud sanctuaries of those spirits tumbling from their barstools, or draped across the juke-box and along the walls, convulsed and twitching like so much Jello. In fact he almost became the "first Black man" to giggle his way to a place among the angels. When the brother reared back and did his thing the gin-induced calm was shattered by a mad fugue euphorically reminiscent of bagpipes, flutes and several neighing horses. It was rumored that if the wind was right you heard the hollerin' and shriekin' way the hell up on Sugar Hill where, if you were feeling down—and the rents had most folks feeling down—you could grab a cab and make the scene before the next lie got told.

Madison Avenue must have heard it too because one day a bespectacled smoothie from CBS showed up with a contract, dangling an impressive amount of bread in return for complete broadcasting rights to the monumental giggle. A studio test was arranged, only as a precautionary step to prepare the sound engineers for the supernatural. But alas, when the broth-er found himself eyeball to eyeball with an unblinking mike he froze. When he got himself together to trigger the giggle, what leaked out was a mousey whimper. The second and third tests were perhaps better, but only if you consider a groaning rabbit

"Bootsie, I don't see why they don't pick a race man to be the vice-president back home. At least they'll know *he* ain't goin' to grab a whole pile of loot because they don't allow race folks to go in most places where they keeps it stashed!"

an improvement over a moaning mouse. CBS didn't. Our man lost absolutely no stature in the community for having struck out his first time at bat; after all most brothers never even got into the line-up. So he settled right back behind his bar and giggled like crazy each time he retold his tale to the world's most appreciative audience.

One night my friend Ted Yates, a local gossip columnist whose violently unsympathetic readers forced him to give it up and study embalming, introduced me to the "Giggler." "Meet my buddy Ollie," said Ted, "he's an artist." The Giggler carefully put down the cocktail glass he was polishing. "He's a WHAT?," he asked. "He's an artist, Man," answered Ted, "draws pictures an' then paints 'em in colors." The Giggler braced himself. "You mean he do that for a livin'?," he whispered, the muscles around his mouth beginning to bump and grind. "That's right," said Ted. "He's a artist by *profession*." CBS should have been there then. The Giggler never got himself together until closing time at five, and by that time he had dropped a dozen glasses. No one will ever know how many male and female Afro-Americans never made it to work the next day due to sore belly muscles.

But not everyone fell out over the idea. Harlemites are very kind people really. Most folks said nothing but simply raised their eyebrows with that expression which clearly says, "Man! Why don't somebody put this poor cat into a straitjacket before he bite somebody!" With Mister Charlie it was another story. The very idea of a Negro (apologies here; that was our official designation then) having the audacity to even think of joining maestros Michelangelo Buonarroti, Rembrandt Van Rijn and Walt Disney, made Charlie mad. Lenny, another Black art student, who regularly regaled us with what he called his POR-TRAIT OF THE ARTIST AS A YOUNG PICKANINNY, explained how he had been alerted to this danger by his father.

"My daddy was a red-dirt sharecropper in fugginassssed

Georgia," explained Lenny. One day Lenny's daddy caught him drawing with a stick of charcoal snatched from the hearth. "He grabbed a big, fat, green switch and tore my backsides loose," Lenny told us. "Whitefolks catch you doin' foolishness like this an' they gon' string yolilllblagggasss up in the tallest tree in Georgia!" A little while later, looking out of the corner of his eye, Lenny saw a glistening tear roll down his daddy's face. The old sharecropper wept silently but when Lenny slipped over and put a skinny arm over his shoulder he jumped up from his stool grumbling, "Better swaller me a spoonful of turpentine an' sugar before this cold turn into the pneumonia!"

My awful comedown at Small's did shake me up but not enough to give me the stutters like poor Sam, the singing waiter who occupied the room next to mine at the Harlem Y. I did develop weird pains in the gut though. Whenever I thought about it I tried to put myself in the Giggler's place. After a while I began to understand. He hadn't been giggling over a little haffassssed nigger wanting to become an artist. He was giggling over all of us. At himself. At all the Black bar-flies who giggled and shrieked with him. He was giggling over the image of old George Washington, who wasn't called "the father of his country" for nothing, tip-toeing around the female slave stables with his pants down. He was giggling over the whole goddamned star spangled lie, and at our Black impotence. In the shadow of the hydra-headed monster you giggle or you cry, and cryin' means dyin'. So I got myself together and climbed back up the Cathedral Parkway Hill to the National Academy of Design.

There was talk then of a Black Renaissance but in muted tones. This was quite fitting because rigor mortis had already set in. During the ludicrously brief lifespan of this American phenomenon a small group of Black poets, novelists and artists did manage to eat fairly regular meals. Black success was doled out and manipulated by a running pack of phoney liberal aristocrats along Park Avenue, Sutton Place and other millionaire slums where, until the new fad took root, white-tied sybarites were swinging from the chandeliers out of mind-bending boredom. Dilettante Carl Van Vechten came to the rescue with his discovery that black is exciting. The bejeweled creeps had a ball. They vied with each other to show off the newest captive Black talent, whom they posed against a background of Currier and Ives prints. Town houses and apartment palaces jumped, once their flagrantly uniformed doormen had been discreetly instructed to keep cool no matter WHAT came in through the front door. Langston Hughes used to tell an unlikely but delicious tale of watching, in open mouthed wonder, a collection of Black talent dip and pirouette with a bevy of lacquered social register harpies in an elegant minuet. A string quartet played Stephen Foster. The Black Renaissance folded when Charlie and Miss Anne discovered some new playthings. The people of Harlem never noticed the difference. Rats continued to chew on infants in side-street flats and cops continued their target practice on the crowded main drags, contributing to U.S. dominance in the Olympic games through the incredible reserves of speed and stamina developed by their intended Black targets.

Funeral services for the Black Renaissance were made bearable by Harlem's Black bartenders. They poured a little extra gin into the glasses of the disillusioned, knowing with their special insights that Black Renaissance can come only from Black people, by Black people, of Black people, and for Black people. And so perhaps with a little extra gin they were only trying to preserve some ex Black talent toward the day when the depth and sweep and human magnificence of unquenchable Black hope produced the inevitable Black Renaissance and ultimately an American people's Renaissance. But who looks for philosophy in a bartender? Which is probably why most Black bartenders keep their mouths shut. Anyway, these musings were rudely interrupted one shimmering Sunday morning in a place called Pearl Harbor.

I never heard of a Black child who wasn't told at some time or other, "Whatever you do don't upset the white folks!" But there was just no place in the home of the brave where a Black kid could reach full growth *without* upsetting the white folks. My friend Walter, from Baltimore, swears that his folks used to take extra precautions by having the kids end their bedtime prayers with, "And please Lord, bless all the white folks." The idea behind this strategy being that the Lord, who obviously had to be white, would pass the word on to Charlie the teacher, Charlie the cop, Charlie the judge, hell, even Charlie the President! And Charlie would put his pistol away and say, "Now there's a family of niggers you can almost trust!" The trouble is you can never know WHAT will upset Charlie. For instance his big brother Sam said, the day after Pearl Harbor, "Every ssswinginnddickkk gon' have to learn to kick and bite, shoot an' fight. In trucks, in jeeps, in tanks and planes, and naturally on your big, fat feet." Predictably this caused some confusion, especially among the more logically minded brothers, who reasoned that since the front of the bus was reserved for Charlie he would insist on the same privilege at the front. Wrong again, Baby!

I saw one brother face his moment of truth at Camp Patrick Henry, our embarkation center. We'd been standing since two in the morning in swirling sleet mixed with snow. The ground in the immense forest was glazed with ice. The barracks bags and other equipment on our backs would have made equilibrium a joke even on solid ground. About five we got the word to move. A tall lean brother who'd fallen at least ten times gave it up and started dragging his barracks bag. Red-faced and nasty, a little ninety-day wonder planted himself in front of the exasperated warrior. "Soldier," he squeaked in what he'd been led to believe was the voice of command, "do you realize that there is Uncle Sam's property you are dragging through that mud?" The brother gazed down at him for a very long and very sad moment before raising his head toward a frigid heaven. The sleet on his helmet was just beginning to reflect the eerie pre-dawn light. Then he said very softly, "Ah shore tore mahhasss when ah raised mah right hand." Adjusting the collar of his field jacket against the freezing drip from his helmet, he calmly curved around the speechless redneck and headed for the war . . . still dragging Uncle Sam's property through the mud.

In 1945 everyone thought that peace really meant peace. Everyone, that is, who didn't live in a ghetto, where peace means burial parlor. Newspapers were amazingly vague about the wave of lynchings sweeping the South. Reporters and police authorities seemed mystified by the number of burned, black corpses hanging in some of the choicest wooded areas, many of them castrated. The supposition was that they were put there by "anonymous persons." Even more mystifying was the fact that they were usually veterans. Dabney, the enigmatic chef behind the soul food counter at the Harlem Moon observed that, "What you all have went and did is upset the white folks." Hell, here we go again. In spite of all that fightinfugginanfoot-racing in North Africa and Italy and in the Pacific, in spite of all that praying that Walter's family had been doing down in Baltimore, Charlie was upset one more time. It's no wonder that one of Dabney's customers had rudely said: "Well FUCK Charlie! And fuck you too, Dabney!"

Now although one was inclined to sympathize with the irate customer's sentiments Dabney did have a point. Charlie was upset again and what seems to have upset him was the fact that Sam had trained two million black youths in the maintenance, handling and angry use of Charlie's most dependable guarantor of life, liberty and the pursuit of happiness for *some* of the people *all* of the time. Sam himself had diligently trained Black youngsters to use rifles, machine-guns and flamethrowers. Some had even flown fighter planes and bombing planes. But what really bugged the judges, sheriffs and southern senators was that these Black soldiers had aimed their contrivances with evil intent at white men! Sure, perhaps there were SS men who'd bashed the pulsating brains out of Jewish infants, or panzer troops who'd mowed down swarms of chained Slovaks. But what mattered most was that these Blacks had killed white men. And to the traditional American way of viewing these things, "Any god damned nigger who raises even a hand against a white man is attempting to overthrow decency—and government—by force and violence." In 1946, 1947, 1948, the "silent majority" was surprisingly loquacious and the word was "put the Blacks in their places." There may just have been some connection between this slogan and the growing number of "anonymously lynched."

But not only Blacks were upsetting Charlie's delicately balanced tranquility. Reds hadn't acted right either. In 1941 when Hitler unleashed his blitzkrieg against the Soviet Union, his generals anticipating Muhammad Ali, who was then in knee pants, boasted, "Three—no later than six." What they meant of course was three weeks. Six at the latest. Every military expert in the United States, from General George Marshall to Walter Winchell went along with this prediction with an eyebrow-raising amount of enthusiasm. Nothing of the sort happened. What did happen four years later was Stalingrad which obviously made the Nazi generals very unhappy. But for some strange reason—at least to the ghetto mind it was strange—it made the top U.S. military and business brass unhappy too! And so the same sheriffs, judges, senators and at least one president screamed that not only the Blacks had to be put in their place—but the Reds too! "And that," observed the irrepressible Dabney, stirring up a mess of steamingly succulent hog maws, "is where the stuff hit the fan." This subversive statement was immediately but discreetly jotted down by a barfly known as Attorney W. Carver Thomas who was later unhappily exposed as Senator Joseph McCarthy's cullud boy in Harlem.

Brother Dabney never connected this humble observation with the exasperating electronic disturbances which began to afflict his home telephone from that time on. In all fairness though, it should be established that the cacophonic disturbances were considerably modified after the senator was pulled off the job and the operation was inherited successively by the FBI, CIA, Army Intelligence, Navy Intelligence, Air Force Intelligence and most recently by the Republican Committee for the Re-Election of the President.

There's an amazing amount of intuition in ghetto circles and something in the climate suggested that Dabney was a marked man. There were rumors to the effect that "the Man suspicioned" that poor old Dabney was not only Black but Red too. Which may account for the remark made by Speedy, the jitney driver who said, "Whitey aint only color conscious like they say. Man, that summbitch is color CRAZY!"

Looking back on those sorry times one sees clearly that Speedy was making more sense than all the think tanks spread across the country. But Sam didn't have to work up a sweat explaining why Blacks had to be put back in their places. All "freedom lovin'" Americans KNEW that. It was because they WERE Black. And it would be silly to forget that a lot of Blacks also fell for the swindle, as evidenced by the fact that the first Blacks to acquire their own swimming pools also happened to be the makers of INSTANT LEMON SKIN BLEACH and DEAD ON CONK.

The "Commissioner," a retired Customs Department porter, could be found sitting on the park bench opposite 555 Edgecombe almost any sunny morning. From this observation post he faithfully imparted "inside stuff" to any brother or sister who had the time to listen. "Now young feller, I am honor bound not to reveal any guvmint secrets," was the Commissioner's invariable opener, "but there's a few things the Folks got to know." He'd then check over both shoulders before continuing in a conspiratorial whisper. "All them Caucasians with tongue twistin' names thats gittin' off the boats every day. Well before the Man gives 'em their naturalization papers they got to recite this here poem. Dont matter none if it's in English or their own language, the Man understand ALL languages. This is what they got to recite:

A chicken aint nothin' but a bird
An' a nigger aint nothin' but a turd.

"But that aint all Man, listen to this. Soon as they comply with that regulation they becomes first class citizens. Then they hops over to the Office of Equal Opportunity an' borrows enough bread to buy 'em a store here in Harlem. Now they know they can charge niggers anything they wants to. First thing you know they done bought a es-tate out on Long Island. He joins the Ku Klux Klan. She joins the Daughters of the American Revolution. They then buys the Stars an' Stripes to hang up over their kidney-shaped swimmin' pool. Now ainthatabitch?"

Charlie has not been called a "color crazy summbitch" for nothing. Ask any surviving American Indian about his relationship with the Great White Father and you've got a real Freudian mess on your hands. Ask any Brown Puerto Rican-American or Yellow Nisei-American if he's ever gotten a fair shake from the Great Society and you can get cut. Don't even bother to bug a soul brother with such inanities!

If it hadn't been for the passion for "notoriety" and bread which throbbed beneath the campaign ribbons of several top military gentlemen the ghettos would never have been hip to the greatest lynching of all time which was in the planning stage in 1947. And of course lynching is a subject of no small interest in the ghetto. At that time, several now defunct publications like *Look* and *Life* were real hung-up on memoirs—

especially the memoirs of the generals who were petulantly feuding over which one had actually won World War II. The cat was let out of the bag when it was realized that there was one subject upon which all of the generals were in surprising agreement. This was the planned "nuclearization of Red Russia." Although it was top, top, secret stuff you could buy it on any newsstand for fifteen cents! (The cost then of *Life* and *Look*.) It wasn't surprising that the brothers were interested since they had been briefed by several street-corner speakers (before the cops fractured their skulls) that the Soviet Union was a nation of brown, yellow and white people, completely and harmoniously integrated. There were some brothers like turban-topped Swami, who usually held the crowd spellbound on 125th and Seventh for hours at a time, who swore that the joyous "miscegenation" of the Russians was THE reason for what Charlie was "fixin' to do"!

Ordinarily the brothers didn't take such a direct approach to what was being put down since at that time Tom still felt safe in the ghetto streets. A favorite spot for signifyin' rappin' was Skippy's Rib Joint over on Eighth Avenue. The distinguished pedagogical emeritus at Skippy's was the "Professor." The Professor may have had another name but I never remember having heard it. What he did have was an encyclopedia which, according to the grapevine, he'd memorized. Even so he always carried it "just in case."

I happened to be in Skippy's one day when one of the brothers mentioned collard greens. The Professor turned to the brother. "Did I hear you mention the name collard greens?" asked the Professor.

"Professor," said the brother, "you aint only heard the word collards but if you put your ear 'long side my gut you can hear 'em growling."

The Professor sort of smiled tolerantly and said, "Don't you realize there aint no such thing in nature called collards?"

"Now cut out the crap, Fess. I know I just had some great collards over at Ma Scruggs'!"

The Professor looked down at his pointed patent leathers for a moment of learned contemplation, and then he said, "I'm sorry to expose your ignorance to the gaze of all these learned gents, but what you just ett and didn't even have sense enough to know what you was eatin' was the tears of Lycurgus, king of the Thracian Edonians, which in case you do not dig, was ancient Greek!"

"Whaaaaat!", gasped the brother.

"Now wait a minute, I aint finished," the Professor commanded. "Lycurgus' tears fell on the ground and sprung up cabbages. . . ."

"Hold it right there Fess. I know damn well I did not eat no cabbage."

"Oh yes you did. Cabbages, or Brassica oleracea variety capitata acephala, which also include kale and collards. That's what you ett. You just had a platterful of Brassica oleracea var. capitata acephala, brother!"

The crestfallen gourmet turned to the bartender and said, "Whew! That mother is DEEP!"

Everybody had a drink including the bartender who then asked, "Hey Fess, what's all this crap about the white folks gettin' ready to drop the THING on the Russians?"

The Professor pushed his sun glasses further down his nose to get a better look at his chastened audience. "You talkin' about the domino theory," he said. "Well, it's like this. This downtown Wall Street cat, name of John Foster Dulles. He went and volunteered to be the Secretary of the State. In that capacity he been conductin' some top secret experiments where he done found out that if you pushes one domino over on top of some other dominoes, they gon' topple over too!"

The bartender gazed at the Professor for several seconds. Then he blurted, "Look Professor, I thought you said he was a

Wall Street man. Now what a Wall Street man doin' fuggggin-nnarounnn with some dominoes?"

"My man," answered the Professor, "You done just asked the sixty-fo' dollar question!"

"Great jumpin' junipers, Brother Bootsie, ain't this mad? I told 'em I wuz Sugar Ray Robinson. Who did you tell 'em you wuz?"

Look Homeward Baby

A large number of the brothers stayed on in Europe after the armistice. I think the main reason was that they couldn't ever again accept being cooped up in ghettos. The ghetto isn't only meant to restrict the movement and growth of bodies. It's also been deliberately organized to stultify and even to deform black minds. When Sam's draft boards began mailing out those "greetings" to the brothers they also unwittingly enclosed the jailhouse keys. These escapees from the land of "freedom and justice for all" were particularly welcomed by the French people, who seem never to have forgotten that during World War I the American commander General Pershing refused to have anything to do with allowing black Americans to shoot and bayonet white Germans. But the French were up-tight and fighting for their lives. General Foch very gratefully accepted the four black American infantry regiments. These proved to be so effective that all of them received the highest French war-time decorations.

Paris of course was the main attraction. But there is something about picking up stakes and moving on that never really seems to work out. The restlessness which compels so many humans to go see what's on the other side of the hill, or river, is self-defeating. There are so many hills and so many rivers. And in the end one sits on some cold stone under an improbable tree and sings the blues. Naturally a Paris boulevard is just about the last place to ever think of singing the blues and so the Black exile does the next best thing. He takes the Metro to the foothills of Montmartre where he will find Leroy Haynes, himself an exile, who will fix any brother or sister with generous helpings of chitlins with collard greens, red beans and rice, and even corn bread! Haynes with his restaurant has struggled valiantly with this problem of nostalgia and in the process has come up with an assortment of chili-based condiments. The most famous of these are called Big Brother and Little Sister. For those who prefer a "mild" condiment Haynes recommends

57

Little Sister. What he evidently means is that a drop or two of Little Sister on the hawg maws need not necessarily remind the diner of the recent film *Is Paris Burning*? But Haynes honestly makes no such claims for Big Brother which he frankly states "is for folks who really dig hot stuff." I have overheard groups of Black surgeons, who'd taxied up to Haynes' between planes from Orly, observe that even a layman must notice that ONE DROP of Big Brother caused a rather alarming protruding of the eyeballs accompanied by a quickening of the respiration which should not be confused with the process of breathing! Obviously what Haynes had in mind when he concocted these diabolical sauces was a surcease of nostalgia. But in fact it is more like curing heartburn by smashing one's big toe with a sledge hammer.

These observations are not meant to imply that Black expatriates, especially painters and sculptors, are unhappy in Europe, especially in France. The art community in Paris, for example, is a completely open one. The only criterion is, are you a good artist? Or at least are you working like hell to become one? Such a criterion induces an atmosphere of camaraderie, a sharing of ideas, techniques, and often soup, all of which seem indispensable in the making of an artist. I never even remotely experienced anything like that at "home" except perhaps in Harlem among a group of really beautiful human beings and artists like the late Augusta Savage, or like Aaron Douglas, Ernie Crichlow, Elton Fax, Romare Bearden and Bob Pious. There is another quality which made Paris a truly civilized place and that was the fact that it was no disgrace to be poor and unsuccessful, with all of the abominable things that word implies in the rat-race society of the "silent majority." At least that was Paris when I arrived in 1951. There's no doubt but that without this liberté, égalité and fraternité there could not have been a Monet, Modigliani, Picasso, or Giacometti. And there certainly could not have been a Henry Tanner, that great Black master whose paintings hang alongside the greats of France in the Louvre, although he is virtually unknown in his native Philadelphia. If this sounds like Paradise forgive me. It isn't, there are pitfalls. But later. . . .

I sort of stumbled on the Cafe Monaco not long after I got to Paris. I'd been wandering through a maze of incredibly narrow streets in the Latin Quarter which couldn't have changed since the time of Rabelais. From the outside there was nothing even remotely seductive about the cafe. As a matter of fact it seemed seedy. But in the murky interior I noticed a tall Black brother sitting with his back against the far wall. Although it was obvious that the sun had never shone in that street since it stopped being a cowrun down to the nearby Seine, the contemplative brother was wearing seemingly opaque sunglasses. What really grabbed me though was the rest of his togs. The main focus was at the top, a black leather cap. Then followed a black turtleneck sweater, black suit under a black overcoat—although it was July—black shoes and socks. I walked in, found myself a small table and ordered a beer. The brother never turned his head and if he ever batted an eye behind those glasses you wouldn't know it without an x-ray machine. After about an hour, and still never turning his head in my direction, the brother whispered, "Where you from, Mon?" That was my introduction to Monsieur Slim Sunday. He was—or had once been—Nigerian. No, he never wore anything but black and he emphasized the fact that his underwear, which he dyed himself, was also black! He never sat with his back to anybody's door or window. "I got no trust, Mon," he explained.

The Monaco was a typical French working-class cafe which noisily raised its sheetmetal shutters at seven when the local clientele, butchers, bakers, hairdressers and little craftsmen, would begin drifting in looking for their cafe au lait, laced with cognac. They would look in again four or five times during the day for some additional fuel—usually vin blanc or rouge—until knocking-off time.

About nine every morning a radiantly angelic and obviously American girl would skip in and take her favorite seat, smiling at the morning like one of Raphael's virgins. There were always ten or twelve little saucers stacked up in front of her on the marble-topped table and I figured she played some kind of expatriate game until I asked one of the brothers. "Well, that's the only way the waiter can keep the count," was the way he explained it to me. I had to ask what kind of a count the waiter was keeping. He stared at me, "You don't know? Where you been, Baby? Well, that's little Julie and she been stoned for near 'bout two years. Every one of them saucers represent one rum!" Later, I learned that little Julie's father was, in the words of another brother, "real big shit at one of them Ivy League colleges when he ain't down in Washington helpin' the President to fuck up foreign policy." Julie sat there with her stack of saucers for another year or so and then one morning she wasn't there. Gone back to New England, they said. About six months later we heard that little Julie had hanged herself. "The trouble wid Julie," explained Ula, the Danish girl whose specialty was gin with beer chasers, "was she wass a decent kid. She couldn' stand dat shiddouse hypocrits wass sellin' in dat fugginnn-American collitch. So she stayed stoned!" I guess little Julie forgot to stay stoned.

The Monaco was something the likes of which had never been seen in the "land of the free." The word to describe it was "harmony." There were the regular French patrons and there were *les amis*. Of these, half were American, about 20 of these were brothers. The rest were English, Canadian, Swedish, a few Danes, one Czech, one Nigerian, two Senegalese and one Indian "untouchable." "All these beautiful s.o.b.'s are here trying to become human beings," explained the ex-cowboy who sat in the window seat all day making quick sketches of everyone who came in. There was a jukebox but it seemed that the only thing anyone ever wanted to hear was "Pops" (Armstrong) singing:

> I see friends shakin hands
> Sayin how do you do
> What they're really sayin
> Is I love you.

There were quite a number of U.S. bases spread about the French countryside in those days which were not the spiritually uplifting places their commanders claimed them to be in their reports to the Pentagon. The more decent GI's couldn't wait to get the hell out on weekends and quite a few dug what was happening in Monaco. The base security sections were considerably less than pleased with the idea of exposing clean-cut and freedom-loving American youths to the Left Bank with its "French immorality" or "treasonable niggers." This probably accounted for the two or three flamboyantly inconspicuous "journalists" who joined the Monaco family.

Another kind of bloodhound eventually showed up, sniffing around the tables and grinning lasciviously. An outlay of a few pre-inflationary dollars to cover the price of vin rouge and beers for some of the cafe's thirsting brothers unearthed enough life stories—invented on the spot—for him to fill out a prefabricated masterpiece called *The Black Expatriate*, which eventually surfaced in a well-known news magazine.[1] One could say that in spite of its clumsily concealed liberal racist paranoia, the cover story was "a step forward." But only because Black Americans hadn't yet been discovered in the United States as people! Yet it would be safe to assume that the main inspiration for its appearance was a dearth of news. Pickings in the heap of human chaos which usually inspires what William Randolph Hearst called "great American journalism" were scrawny. There were no earthquakes, famines or train wrecks. Billion dollar bank heists had dried up on the editors and of course airplane hijacking hadn't yet been invented. The foreign news section dozed in the same post-war atmosphere which led most otherwise mentally capable world leaders to conclude that the "natives" of the world had forgotten the promises of freedom made in the heat of battle. This serenity, which is the bogeyman in the lives of advertising and circulation vice presidents, presented the Paris correspondent with a chance to do his thing. Result *The Black Expatriate*.

It wasn't that the piece was offensive, or at least no more so than the usual Anglo-Saxon, myopic view of things which aren't well bred enough to go out and drop dead. But it definitely exuded the unmistakable bouquet of Establishment disdain despite its well-educated admission that Paris had always lured expatriates. There were even American expatriates like Benjamin Franklin, Edgar Allan Poe, F. Scott Fitzgerald, Hemingway and Henry Miller. But the real message was that any brother who hinted, by taking off, that God's country could contain anything unpalatable was messing around with subversion, if not outright treason!

Eventually the number containing the article found its way to Monaco, where Dick Wright read it to the gleefully agitated crowd with more than his usual gusto, punctuating each lamentably ill-informed fact with, "Keeee-ryess, now ain't thatabitch?" Chicago George spasmodically stamping both feet and giggling, fell out. "Expatriate," he shrieked. "Sheeeeee-ittt, them mothahs ain't even 'lowed me to be a patriot so hownafuggg I'm gon' git to be a EX-patriot?"

Some afternoons when I'd finished work I'd stroll over to Montparnasse hoping to find Harris. Brother Harris was unadulterated "country," from praying on his knees every night before hopping into the sack, to making clicking noises when the cussing got to be too colorful for his AME Sunday school background. Harris had never even been to the town *next* to his in Mississippi when the long arm of the U.S. Army, Mess Section, reached in and plucked him out. Harris had cooked powdered eggs and dehydrated spuds from El Alamein to Anzio, where a red-neck from the 82nd Airborne, perhaps believing that Black brothers deserved Purple Hearts more than most folks, shot Harris in his right buttock. When the war ended Harris had convinced himself that it was God who'd plucked him out of good ole Mississippi and so damned if he wasn't going to show God his appreciation by staying out! Harris also had a theory. "I never seen no diff'rence 'tween them SS and these airborne," Harris explained in his gentle voice. "They even looks alike an' I have seen 'em buddyin' around together over in the prisoner-of-war compound. You realize what that mean?" I had to admit that I didn't, knowing that Harris was going to tell me anyway. "Well Brother, I'm gon' tell you," said Harris. "It mean that now that this war is over they gon' kiss an' make up. It also mean that when I get back home the best I can do is maybe get me a job out at the white folks country club, an' there *they* be hollerin' 'Harris get me this, and Harris get me that,' an' befo' they go in to play the pinball machines they be wantin' to rub my head fer luck. An' because one of 'em is a nice blue-eyed SS an' the other is a nice blue-eyed airborne, I got to let 'em or else have some trouble with the sheriff. Tha's the American Dream Brother! An' tha's also why Ma Harris' youngest boy is gon' make tracks." Harris was as good as his word. He got himself demobilized in Paris, heard about the GI Education Bill and signed up to study drawing and painting at the Grande Chaumière. It was Herb Gentry and Larry Potter, two Black expatriate painters, who told me between squalls of laughter, about Harris' first day at the Grande Chaumière. Harris had signed up for the "life class" although he didn't quite know exactly what that meant. He found a seat in the huge studio and did what everyone else was doing. He opened his large drawing pad, steadying it on the chair in front, opened his box of brand new charcoal pencils and erasers and then looking up, realized that there was a completely nude woman standing on the platform just above him in the first pose of the afternoon. Harris split, leaving all of his equipment and his most prized possession, his beret. He didn't stop galloping until he'd locked the door of his tiny hotel room in the Rue Delambre! "Thought the rednecks had finally trapped him" gasped Gentry, wiping the laughing tears from his eyes. It took a week to convince Harris that the French didn't have any rednecks, and so Harris cautiously went back. Of course everyone knew that Harris would never become even a third rate painter but he was so beamingly happy that not even the instructors had the heart to tell him.

I usually found Harris around three or four in the afternoon at the Cafe Select in the Boulevard Montparnasse, where we'd discuss art and what Harris called "deep stuff" until dinner time. One rainy afternoon I poked my head in, looking down toward the corner table where Harris usually roosted with his drawing portfolio in the seat of the wicker chair beside him, his broad forehead puckered over some book of reproductions. As usual, Harris was there, but he didn't jump up and wave enthusiastically as he customarily did. I walked toward his table, shaking the rain from my "impermiable." Before I reached the table I realized that there were tears streaming down Harris' face. The old waiter Ramon stood nearby, staring at Harris, his usually genial face twisted in anguish. I questioned Ramon with my eyes but he just lifted his shoulders in that most expressive French gesture which says "je ne sais pas" (I don't know). I sat down opposite Harris who seemed unable to speak. "Jesus Christ, Harris, what's happening?" I asked. Harris roughly wiped one side of his face with his sleeve. After a while he looked up and growled, "This is what the bastards have did to me!" I guess hearing Harris curse for the first time shook me up more than the tears and so I asked who had done what. "All of 'em. Every lousy-assed one of 'em goddamit," he hissed. I ordered a couple of beers and ham sandwiches from Ramon, who seemed reluctant to leave Harris' side. Then Harris told me the story.

He'd been walking along the boulevard casually looking into the gay shop windows. It hadn't started to rain yet and the streets glowed in that exhilarating luminosity which exists only in Paris. Harris remembered that he'd felt "happier than a Baptist preacher at a banquet of fried catfish and cornbread." He stood in front of a gift shop looking at the seductive objects on display and after several moments he realized that there was a girl standing beside him looking at some green crystal glasses. He could see her face reflected in the clear plate glass but then he caught his breath. The reflection was smiling directly at him. Harris turned in the other direction automatically, thinking that the girl was smiling at someone else. But there was no one else. She was small and very pretty, hugging a steno notebook under one arm. Harris gulped when the girl turned from the window and smiled directly at him before she turned to walk slowly toward the Rue Vavin bus stop with a mesmerized Harris trailing after her. When the 85 bus arrived she stepped up to the platform, still smiling. Harris froze. He simply could not follow her into the bus "like I know she wanted me to." The girl seemed puzzled but stepped down quickly before the doors shut and several bored passengers quipped remarks about people not making up their minds. The girl walked slowly toward the Metro station, turning again to smile encouragement at Harris. Reaching the green rococo Metro sign she began to descend the stairs and when she was sure that Harris was still there she handed her metro ticket to the collector, who punched it and reached over her shoulder for the next, which should have been Harris but Harris was already racing trembling back up the steps to the Boulevard. He'd been sitting for more than an hour in the Select while the sky darkened and the rain slashed down, groaning, "That's what the dirty bastards have did to poor old Harris!"

In the twenty-two years of what some people insist on calling "self-exile," I've lived or made long visits to many places, from the southern tip of Sicily to the hauntingly beautiful north of Sweden. And in all that time and in all those places I've never felt that I was an exile. Or perhaps one might say that Black people are all exiles unless they're African people living in Africa. I'm fairly well convinced that one is an exile only when one is not allowed to live in reasonable peace and dignity as a human being among other human beings. Where one can give love and respect and receive the same from one's neighbors one is no exile. Where one can even get pissed off with the god damned neighbors just as the neighbors will get pissed off with us at times—because we're humans and not angels. I remember expressing something similar late one night in a place called the Mars Club in Paris, when Beauford Delaney said, "Brothers, who knows. Maybe the angels get pissed off with one another too. After all, we don't know what goes on on the *other side*." And pianist Art Simmons banged his whiskey glass down and solemnly intoned, "You know something else brother, I DON'T WANT TO KNOW!"

Whenever I rap with myself over this question of exile I remember Harris' theory about the SS and the airborne cats giving him a hard time IF he'd goofed and returned to Mississippi to flunkey out at the country club. Who would be the exile, the now naturalized SS cat—or Harris? Do I hear you say it's a set-up example? Okay. Let's just drop the SS part and select a less abstract example. Let's say Wernher von Braun, now a solidly integrated part of the Establishment (Alabama section). Do you think for one moment that Hitler's monstrously effective V-bomb expert has ever been barred from any Alabama country club, or got busted in the mouth by a sadistic sheriff like

ANY Black American who fought on OUR side? Hell no! And do you think that Herr Von This and Herr Von That don't have thousands of Harrises to serve them hand and foot—and maybe get their heads rubbed for luck in the bargain? Isn't THIS the American Dream? Well who in the hell is the exile? Certainly not von Braun. He's among his own having a ball. And not Harris either. He's still in Paris, selling a drawing now and then, or working out at the Renault automobile plant occasionally, and living among PEOPLE who love him because he's a thoroughly lovable human being.

Still, there are only two kinds of people in Europe where I fully experienced this *complete* human integration. They were Russian people and French people. I admit that I spent only two and a half months in the Soviet Union, as a guest of the Soviet satirical magazine *Krokodil*. In that space of time I traveled from Leningrad to Tashkent sketching, talking, drinking and laughing, and once in an open decked bus on the twisting road up to Lake Ritza, in the Caucasus, I sang along with the Russian tourists. They were city folks and peasant folk with a sprinkling of vacationing Soviet GIs and their wives or girl friends. Hell, I didn't know the words of their spontaneous songs, but I knew the music and I sensed the immense generous heart beating beneath that music, sometimes gay, sometimes plaintive, always human. And as those people realized that I had joined their singing—and it was a thoroughly unconscious act—I saw the tears well up in many eyes and a shimmering light seemed to completely envelope that bus. We'd reached a dizzying height—and it had nothing to do with mountains.

Twelve of those "exile" years I spent in France and as a result I can only say that I love the French people. Above all I love and deeply admire the French working class, its proudly working class artists, poets and other intellectuals, and when all is said and done, these are THE French people. THEY are France. But space doesn't permit me to do justice to this subject.

Last summer, the summer of 1972, John Pittman one of the editors of the *Daily World* wrote me from New York suggesting that I grab a flight and pay them a visit in September. I'd been very, very happily turning out two political cartoons each week for the *Daily World* and it seemed that the arrangement was mutually rewarding. It's alright to live in Europe drawing and painting for personal satisfaction while turning out illustrations and cartoons for European publications for porkchops, but there is something missing somehow. I'm Black, and my people are engaged in a difficult and heroic struggle for freedom. While this is a worldwide struggle of oppressed people against the injustice and savage brutality which seem to be essential weapons for the maintenance of capitalism, my personal part of that struggle seems inseparably bound to how that struggle is being waged in the United States. Although I believe that "art for art's sake" has its merits, I personally feel that my art must be involved, and the most profound involvement must be with the Black liberation struggle. My cartoon character Bootsie has been a part of that struggle for 39 years and I believe, as Langston Hughes did, that satire and humor can often make dents where sawed-off billiard sticks can't. In 1968, when John invited me to become a part of the *Daily World* staff I felt that here was an opportunity to really get some licks in. I've often gotten letters from friends asking me how I manage to keep up with what's being put down in the USA when I've lived for so long in Europe. I can only think of that very corny reply: "You can take the boy out of the country but you can't take the country out of the boy." But things do change in twenty-one years and I felt that it would do me a lot of good to see it. I took the leap in September fortified by Czechoslovakian beer, the best in the world as far as I'm concerned. Furthermore you can have as much as you want on Czech Airlines, which is the one I took. Thus fortified, by the time the pilot announced that we were forty thousand feet above Newfoundland on the last leg to Kennedy, I'd managed to get on top of my conflicting emotions to such a degree that I found myself chuckling to the music going around in my head, which was "Pops'" incomparable growling of *Bill Bailey Won't You Please Come Home*!

Dorothy Robinson, that great soul sister, who is business manager of the *Daily World* came out to Kennedy to meet me accompanied by her sister. Dorothy and I had never met and so she'd provided herself with a photograph which her sister apparently hadn't seen because when we finally "linked-up" Sis said, "Baby, I had NO IDEA you were black," and throwing both arms around my neck she said, "Welcome home, Sugar!" That did it. I WAS home. I was with PEOPLE. I was also in the midst of a different civilization from the one I'd left just a few hours ago, I began to realize as we zipped along the highway from Kennedy to the Triboro Bridge. This realization grew as I began counting the wrecks scattered along the centerpiece which *sometimes* separates east from west bound traffic. I really couldn't figure out what had been going on since I hadn't had any news of that highway having been accidentally strafed by air force jets. Inevitably my curiosity got the upper hand and so I asked Dorothy about all that twisted metal. Before she could answer Sis said, "Labor Day weekend, Honey," in a tone which implied that ANY idiot should have been hip to that. After a few miles it dawned on me that SOMEBODY was getting something out of this endless scene of disaster. At regular intervals along the freeway there were immense billboards proclaiming the sheer impossibility of enjoying life without a Ford, Plymouth, Cadillac, well, you name it. This was nothing less than psychodelic. There we were whizzing past these chewed up, burnt out metal cadavers on one side; on their backs, on their sides, completely flattened and impossibly twisted. And on the other side were these billboards saying, "Baby, don't let this scene get

---

69

you down. ALL YOU NEED is THIS gleaming 200 m.p.h. monster—and a countdown! EASY CREDIT TERMS AVAIL-ABLE."

When we turned off the Triboro into 135th Street I knew that somebody *up there* had simply been hardening me up for the main event! That kaleidoscopic graveyard of mangled rubber tires and chrome, scorched lacquer, disemboweled hoods and rib-like door frames left behind us was only shadow boxing. Racing crosstown, turning up Lenox to 145th, turning again up the hill to Broadway with the car windows up was like flying at tree-top level through an utterly soundless nightmare. Harlem's harried crowds swirled across streets, streamed along side-walks, through and around poverty's bomb craters of garbage and senseless debris. Brothers, sisters, children, all Black, scampered or teetered on the brink of constant and unseen disaster while the needle-scarred casualties lurched against plate glass or lay spread-eagled half in, half out of weeping doorways. Looming up on all sides were the mummies of slum buildings embalmed and wrapped in rusted sheet metal, street level openings sealed with planks. Staring up at one of these stone ghetto cadavers into its rows of black-windowed-empty-eye-sockets I felt the goose-pimples. It wasn't completely dead. High up in a blackened fifth floor window was a completely motionless figure in a floppy hat and threadbare overcoat. Both of its elbows were propped on the windowsill steadying a pair of binoculars trained, as far as I could see, on nothing! A once blue painted sign nailed up against a murky store front plain-tively boasting THE WORLD'S MOST FASTEST BARBER quickly disappeared as Dorothy swung the wheel and we slid down the hill toward Riverside Drive and the Hudson. We stopped, dou-bleparked and I stared down through the canyon of brown-stones to the river and across to the New Jersey cliffs crenelated with white-gleaming condominium giants where Charlie and Miss Anne sat on their Babylonian terraces gleefully regarding the terrible revenge exacted against those who'd dared to hope. With the binoculars of my mind I imagined them sipping their six martinis and gradually sliding down their reclining chairs to the red tiles slowly turning amber. Charlie's overworked bladder released his stored-up piss to form a Rorschach easily identified as THE AMERICAN DREAM. Sure, Charlie had put the "niggers in their place," as he had put the Indians in theirs, and as his paid mercenaries were obediently applying the formula all over Indo-China. At least, that is what he stupidly thought.

A few days later, on my way to visit old friends in Vermont the train slithered into a bleakly lit station. I'd been dozing and when the discreet squealing of the brakes jerked me awake I looked at my wristwatch. It was three AM and there were wisps of fog swirling along the vapored window panes. Outside in the gloomy light filtering through the windows there was this cat weaving under his load of Old Grand Dad or something. He'd evidently climbed down out of one of the train's rear cars and was stumbling along just outside my window. A blurry white face was turned up to me and I saw the mouth move soundlessly. I shoved the window up a bit and he teetered precariously trying to focus. Then he pointed his finger at me and I heard him ask, "Shhhay buddie—WHERE ARE YOU?" I couldn't see a station sign or anything and so I told him that I'd be damned if I knew. He blinked fuzzily for a second, put his head down, mumbling, "God damned fuckin' dumb nigger," and staggered off into the darkness, presumably back to his own coach. Now I knew where I was. I was home Baby!

But home wasn't what it used to be. There HAD been some changes made. My old and very dear friends Henry Winston and Jim Jackson, along with John Pittman, had brought up the notion of my helping out in the circulation drive the *Daily World* was putting on. This meant traveling around the country a bit. "It would be a great opportunity for you to get the feel of things again," Winnie suggested which I realized was absolutely true, not only for grabbing hold of what's been happening but there'd also be the visual thing which, of course, is extremely important to a graphic artist.

A week later I was in Nashville. Now let me tell you about Nashville in 1948, the last time I was there. My job then was public relations director in the national office of the NAACP in New York, a post I'd accepted after much soul-searching. It was terribly difficult giving up art but one day when I'd heard about the South Carolina cops gouging out both eyes of a Black veteran, Isaac Woodard, that ended the debate. Or as my wartime buddies used to say, "That's all she wrote!" But sitting in a beautifully appointed office in West 40th Street watching the pigeons do their thing atop the classical facades of the main New York Public Library tends to develop a lot of fat around the brain. This sad condition was painfully brought to my attention at the Nashville Airport when I scampered into the gleaming Braniff DC6, rushed for a window seat and buckled myself in. A few seconds later an elegantly togged lady who seemed to be smelling something very unpleasant, edged into the outside seat. When the stewardess came down the aisle there was a whispered conversation which terminated when the stewardess turned her white mask toward me with the advice that I'd be acting real smart if I got the hell out of that seat and moved up forward. She didn't add "or else" but it was there beneath the words. I moved. I still had enough of my wits left about me to remember that I was, after all, in this greatest of all democracies, Black and outnumbered. You dig? But it turned out much better than I deserved. The only vacant seat left was up front next to a sister who turned out to be so cool, so full of quietly brilliant humor that I almost forgot the honeysuckle-drenched woman who carried the power of the whole U.S. government and its "law" enforcement thugs firmly clutched between her miserably scrawny haunches.

Now here I was, in 1972, twenty-five years later, at the same

Nashville Airport. When I heard my flight being called I took the escalator down to the port boarding room where I took a seat near the door. A few minutes later that same god damned woman came into the room. Of course, when I got myself together I realized that it wasn't she but it sure as hell could have been. Something had happened to Miss Anne in the intervening years. She'd lost that mulishly arrogant canter. Instead of sweeping into the room she trickled in. The megalomaniac White-Fairy-Queen glare, which bestselling novelists describe as "a *level* stare" wasn't working. Instead she wore a simpering plea of helplessness with which she checked the room. I was the only Black passenger in the room and so, naturally, those hypocritically cunning eyes stopped and she moved toward me like the mesmerized lady in *Dracula*. She took the next seat and leaning toward me she said, "Suh, ah sho to goodness hope that nobody in heah is gon' hah-jack our plane this tahm. Do you s'pose they will?" Talk about Bugville. That's where I was at! When I finally got my mouth to close up I wanted to laugh until I cried but when I managed to get myself together I told her, "Well no, Miss Anne, I don't think there's anything to worry about." She smiled even more and hurried to say, "No, I'm Miss Lurleen. . . ." I didn't hear the rest of it because this time the chuckles were breaking through my cool. Seeming somewhat relieved, but not much, Miss Lurleen continued, "Do you reckon anyone in heah is ca'ing a guuuun?" "No," I assured her, "if anybody, you for instance, were carrying a gun in your handbag all these electronic devices around here would start acting like the Fourth of July!" She settled back then and sighed. "Ah do hope you're raht, Sirrrr. It was real nahse talkin' to ya." But I know she was thinking, "If anybody is going to hi-jack this plane it's got to be this Black man. And I really can't rightly put my finger on the 'why'. All I know is that he SHOULD!"

Then there was Chicago and the composite portrait of this new America began to take on form in my mind. The shapes were surrealist, sick, the colors grating and ominous. But there were passages suggesting movement, even dynamic movement, and buried in these masses were flashes of vibrant, even beautiful light. Walking around the Loop, in the grim shadow of the constantly rumbling elevated tracks above, I went into a rambling bar restaurant, one of those quick-service American inventions which are beginning to pollute the relaxed atmosphere and the digestive habits of many European cities. I had a couple of hours to spare before my appointment with Ish Flory, who was a very busy candidate for the Illinois governorship. The fact that Ish was Black AND running on the Communist Party ticket would have brought at least one division of the Illinois National Guard swarming into the Chicago ghetto with live ammunition only a few years ago. Only a few nights before I'd listened to an unbelievably courageous Mr. Flory tell a solidly WASP audience that if they had any sense and real concern for the future of the country they'd realize that they NEEDED men like him in office if only for the fact that they were the only ones who couldn't be indicted for very grand larceny. The WASPS actually applauded—and that was before Watergate!

I walked through the self-service restaurant to the bar and hoisted myself onto a stool where I could watch the World Series in color on the TV set suspended up above the rows of bottled liquid libations, and where I could drink in the movements, also in color, of one of the most beautiful barmaids I'd ever seen on either side of the ocean. She was a sister and the characters at the bar called her Mink, but with the careful air of men handling live ammunition. Mink was as cool as she was striking and she placed the straights and highballs before the mixed clientele with courtesy mixed with an indefinable aura which cautioned the cats, sober or drunk, against asking for anything that wasn't on the alcohol list. A few minutes later, while Sal Bando was busting up the ball game with one over the fence in the tenth inning, a couple of red-neck hardhats came in and grabbed two stools in the midst of the hysteria which had taken over. They ordered a couple of beers, which Mink served up dead-pan but courteously, and began like everyone else to second guess the losing manager's choice of putting in a right-hand pitcher to a left-hand batter. The joint calmed down and the hardhats ordered another round. When Mink stood before them, deftly flicking the spatula to skim off the overflowing foam, one of the hardhats asked if he could pin something on the front of her blouse. The other clients tensed but the hardhats, undoubtedly on another frequency, continued their subtly lascivious program. I heard Mink ask "What is it?" One of the hardhats had a little plastic American flag, the kind which clips into the lapels. In a soft undertone Mink said, "Look Baby, I DON'T WANT IT!" The hardhats tensed. "You sayin' you won't wear YOUR flag?" Tiny and tense, but cool, Mink's low voice cut through the silence like a straight razor. "Mister," she said, "that flag used to be decent but y'all went an' shit on it so much that I DO NOT WANT NO PART OF IT!" The hardhats were incredulous. "You mean— . . . " one of them stuttered. "YES. I mean you go an' clean it up. Then I'll think about it." The other hardhat said, "Love it or leave it." Mink's eyes cracked lightning, "Look Muuurrrfuggger," she hissed, "I ain't lookin' for trouble, see? That's why Saturday is my last day here. Ya wanta know why? 'Cause the other day I had to lay one up side the head of the lousy peckerwood that runs this crappy joint. Dig?" The thoroughly confused hardhats jerked back from the bar and one of them said whiningly, "But the American flag. . . ." "You heard me," said Mink. "It's because of phoney shits like you hardhats that every time I sees a picket line I get on it. And I don't care WHAT the fuck they picketin' about!" The hardhats sat staring at their half-emptied beer glasses and then when they felt that no one was looking at them they slunk out shaking their heads sadly. A half hour later when I met Ish I asked him if he needed someone for a picketline. Then I told him about Mink and the hardhats. Ish listened with that enigmatical grin of his, his laughing eyes half-shut as if he were tasting a rare wine. "Ollie," he mused, "these sisters are something else. There are sisters like the one you're telling me about all over this land and when the MAN looks into their eyes he KNOWS they ain't playing."

Earlier in this article I wrote of the sad history of a so-called Black Renaissance, tragically aborted because it was neither Black nor a Renaissance. Traveling through the betrayed American cities last autumn I became aware of a profound trembling of the earth in every ghetto. Young Black people with amazingly straight backs, knowing, or better still, *convinced* that Black IS beautiful too are now enabled to release the blindingly creative energies which have always been bound in chains by a criminally bigoted system. A revolution is taking place in the ghettos if one has the eyes to look behind the frightening facade. And revolutions require expression. Black kids painting huge murals on discouragingly neglected slum buildings are expressing that revolution. Sidestreet theatres, poetry readings, and neighborhood museums are part of that expression. They're all expressing ideas with which Black people can identify. A Black Renaissance has already been born.

But don't think that Charlie's wall of lies hemming in the ghetto is impenetrable. People, especially young white people, in America and in Europe are aware of what's happening in the ghetto even if their fathers maintain an obstinate ignorance. All over Europe I've seen young people who've studied the methods of the Black Liberation movement, applying those same methods to the job of forcing a bit of humanity into their profit-crazed and economically teetering countries. Of course it's got its amusing sides too and very often one is forced to rush somewhere for a drink after he's seen a group of the blond German youths with hair frizzled and worn in Afros. The parents of these kids have all picked the portrait of the President of the United States as a symbol of what was good in America. If anyone recognized Nixon's portrait today he probably wouldn't admit it. But I've been in no part of Europe where there wasn't the picture of a *good* American—and it was always Angela Davis!

NOTE

1. "Amid the Alien Corn," *Time*, 72 (November 17, 1958), 28. See "The Last Days of Richard Wright," note 1, above.

Through Black Eyes

According to the parchments left by Venetian scribes Marco Polo "discovered" China near the end of the 13th century. We may safely assume though that China was there all the time, and not breathlessly waiting to be discovered by Europe either. As a matter of fact a very high civilization had flourished in that land for a thousand years before Signor Polo got around to discovering it, with an official census, postal system, and paper money, four centuries before Polo's colleagues even got around to dreaming of such things. But the Chinese neither looked, spoke nor dressed like Venetians and so what Marco Polo's eyes saw were hordes of slant-eyed, "yellow heathens" lurking behind a wall. He must have seen something else though because soon after his return "Italian" spaghetti, macaroni, noodles and ravioli were invented.

This legacy of "seeing" strange places and even stranger people through eyes like those of Marco Polo, Stanley and Livingston, Kipling, Tarzan and ITT has persistently colored "informed" popular knowledge until well into our own time, always making the business of snatching goodies from their rightful but "heathen" owners more palatable. But in recent times the Establishment has begun to show signs of acute dis-

Review of *Through Black Eyes: Journeys of a Black Artist to East Africa and Russia*. By Elton C. Fax. Dodd, Mead, New York. xi, 203 pages. $6.95.

"No, it dont make no sense to me neither Bootsie. But white
folks jus' wont buy nothin' if it makes sense!"

comfort. The traditional one-eyed view of "natives" has produced some very painful surprises, as General Douglas MacArthur discovered when he set one foot into the Yalu River against the advice of "gong-beating hordes of slant-eyed gooks." Or a few years later in Vietnam when Westmoreland ruefully discovered that what a "slope" bicyclist can and will do to a Sherman tank if he's upset wasn't included in the West Point curriculum. These major losses of—well, let us say—face now seem to be producing a climate of change in "official circles." One of the more nourishing fruits of this change is a remarkable travel book by artist-writer Elton Fax.

Only a few years ago, if "official circles" had been asked to consider a book with the title *Through Black Eyes* the answer would certainly have been "What the hell for?" But times aint like what they used to be—though Charlie still bears watching. On the inside flap of Elton Fax's excellent book one reads, "As an artist and Black man who has spent much of his life in urban slums, Elton Fax brought a finely attuned point of view to his visits to the Black nations of East Africa and to the non-white communities of Soviet Central Asia. His journeys to Uganda, the North Sudan, Ethiopia and Tanzania were arranged by the EDUCATIONAL AND CULTURAL DIVISION OF THE U.S. STATE DEPARTMENT." Not too long ago a blurb like that on any book would have sent the sisters and brothers scurrying for the woods like they had good sense. Today that could be a mistake. It certainly would be a mistake in the case of Fax's newest book.

It must be a bit of a gamble when the State Department subsidizes the journeys of an artist to some far-off place, especially if the artist is a good one. This must be so because the main ingredient for excellence in art is an almost obstinate honesty. Mr. Fax is an EXCELLENT artist. His book is authentic and credible and regardless of what anyone else WANTED him to see, this IS what he saw . . . and felt. The drawings in this book are superb. Some of them, I think, are great drawings, and in a world saturated with photo magazines and TV they establish a human contact which cannot be duplicated in any other way.

Through Black Eyes is literally filled with wonderful anecdotes which breathe life into Fax's descriptions of Black East Africa. These anecdotes are filled with wit and wisdom, and with a subtle humor which will scurry away from you "if you aint with it." One of the things which Mr. Fax's sponsors had in mind, naturally, was that he would "speak" to Africans. Of course there were the "knuckle-head" political attaches who would sort of hint that Fax should tell the Africans what they'd been telling them, "and everything's gon' be all right." But anyone who didn't badly require the services of a shrink could see that things were anything but all right! Of course some very decent officials turned up too. One of them asked Fax what he was going to tell the Africans who asked him about the "race situation" in the U.S. In effect Fax answered, "Well, I'm going to tell it like it is!" The official grabbed Fax's hand and said, "Well thank God somebody realizes that we'd better stop B.S.'ing these people!"

The key to Mr. Fax's success both as artist and as human being (and as State Department envoy—though I doubt they'd realize it) can be found in something he wrote for the preface of his book. Having spent forty-five years of his life *in the urban slums*, he traveled to Mexico, Central and South America, the Caribbean and recently to Africa. In some places he found dedicated, progressive leaders, but he writes, "Wherever I found a preponderance of 'colorful natives,' I found them scrambling for the meanest kind of existence." He also found "sophisticated" leaders and their cliques. And even where these leaders appeared equally as exotic as the masses, "a distinct difference separated them." In the midst of Black African misery these

Black African leaders LIVED WELL. It is at this point that I believe the title *Through Black Eyes* might tend to be a bit misleading.

The "miserable masses" Fax saw—and so beautifully drew—were Black. The greasy-jowled leaders and their cliques were also Black. Did these leaders see these masses through black eyes? I doubt it very much. The fact is they see them through the same eyes as the WHITE COLONIALISTS who were recently prevailed upon to split the African scene! These are THROUGH THE EYES OF RUTHLESS EXPLOITERS. Elton Fax saw these exploited and degraded Africans through the eyes of love, brotherhood . . . and anger. His bitingly perceptive charcoal line and textures labored with compassion literally shout this. But how could it be otherwise? This great artist Elton Fax—this grandson of the most exploited of humans, a slave—this Afro-American who'd had to bite and kick his way up through that most exploited of all patches of earth, a slum ghetto—saw and portrayed the African masses with the eyes of all of those things which he is. Are these BLACK EYES? It would be most curious if they were because they are the same eyes as Indians, Puerto Ricans, Chicanos, Afro-Americans . . . and let's not forget those "po" assed whites in their forgotten slums.

But this is a book of many sides. Not only does Elton Fax supply us with a "like it is," he also provides a "like it was." Before each stop on his journey there is a brief but penetrating historical background of the place and its people. In the section on Ethiopia Fax sounds a warning of things to come (the book was written before the current revolutionary outbreak in that country) and reasons why. In the North Sudan he dissolves one of the gleefully accepted myths of imperialism, that there is an unbridgeable gulf between Arab and Black. But none of the Arabs or Blacks with whom he talked had been told about it, and in fact they were all Black! Their attitude seemed to be, "Hell man, we're ALL Sudanese!" And at one party—after making sure that the State Department gentleman had really left—his Sudanese hosts, roaring with laughter, threw their arms about Fax's shoulders and said, "You know something else, man? YOU'RE SUDANESE TOO!"

Through Black Eyes concludes with a section on Uzbekistan which was a separate trip made after his State Department subsidized trip to Africa. Fax is not at all what one might call a "political" person. For that very reason the section, with the usual beautiful drawings, is extremely interesting. During the cruelly racist rule of the Russian czars, Fax explains, Uzbekistan's "rich coal and iron deposits were made readily available to the French and Belgian operators. The British and French ran the oil wells while the textile mills and other factories were divided among German, French and British capital. It naturally follows that under such an arrangement the condition of the native laborers would be miserable. . . . With the Socialist Revolution of October 1917 came sweeping changes." These striking similarities between colonialism's cruel treatment of brown Uzbeks and Africa's black peoples were not lost on Mr. Fax. Though he doesn't press the point he does make his readers aware of one significant difference. In many of the newly independent African nations the same French, British, Belgian and German exploiters have been replaced by "sophisticated Black exploiters" while in Uzbekistan capitalist exploitation was uprooted by Socialism. If one is honestly interested in finding proof that exploitation and racism can be completely eliminated, here is the proof—with beautiful drawings.

Like Most of Us Kids

In 1865 a young painter in a Munich garret was convinced that painting was a dead end in a one way street—a point of view which has recurred consistently since Michelangelo's Sistine Chapel triumph. Obviously, the Munich painter—who was named Wilhelm Busch by the way—was suffering from a mild form of "artist's depression." I say mild because artists have been known to blow their fuses during these bouts. Van Gogh, for example, had it so bad that he hacked off one of his poverty-wrinkled ears before doing away with himself completely—an act which led to his being "discovered."

Busch apparently wasn't all that strung out. Indeed, he began applying autotherapy, playing around with a series of satirical drawings, usually in four or five panels, featuring two kids named *Max und Moritz*. Not only had Busch embarked upon a new and highly successful career, but he'd also invented the cartoon strip.

Inevitably, the cartoon strip arrived in America where it was called the "comic" strip, although anyone who can find any humor in the great majority of them in our modern and allegedly more advanced times could only be a Jack the Ripper or a Boston Strangler. Today's comic strip artists dump more

Review of *Luther's Got Class*. By Brumsic Brandon Jr. Paul S. Eriksson, Inc., New York. Unpaged. $3.95 (paper).

"Oooh look, Sis, a robin red breast, and it must be spring. Do you reckon Uncle Bootsie was lying when he said spring comes three weeks earlier over 'cross town where the white folks live?"

chauvinism, vicious racism, kinky sex, torture and horror into the inner recesses of American brain tissue—young and old—than any other known carrier of disease. Fortunately there are exceptions. One very great exception is Brumsic Brandon, Jr.

The American comic strip—but let's call them cartoon strips—is BIG business. The cartoonists work under contract to a small number of monopolies called syndicates, and their strips are distributed daily to thousands of newspapers all over the world. Naturally, the artists are exceptionally talented and the financial rewards are exceptional—which of course makes Brandon even more exceptional because he's not only a brilliant cartoonist but also a Black one! Until his arrival, syndicate doors were firmly barred against Black cartoonists. The reasons for this should be obvious. First, it is an extremely competitive field and, secondly, those who make it earn more than the average upper middle class businessman; even much more than, let's say, the Grand Wizard of the Ku Klux Klan! In spite of public relations triumphs like *New Frontier*, *The Great Society*, *Prayin' an' Stickin' Together*, etc., Charlie's U.S. is racist and class oriented. So what's that got to do with comic strips? Well like we've already seen, the MAN owns them all (remember those syndicates) and like we all know, every decent American kid will fight his parents like a tiger to get at the Sunday comics before they do. If he loses the battle he'll rush into his room where he's got so many HORROR COMICS stashed under his bed that the bedsprings can't spring. And what the whole family gets out of all this is a sense of "them" and "us." Us naturally being the nice decent folks in places like Grand Rapids or Plains, Georgia. I won't waste any typewriter ribbon explaining who "them" is.

Why then would the syndicates open their doors wide enough to let a Black cartoon in? That answer can be found in your old copies of FREEDOMWAYS. I'll only say this: It all began when a little Black lady who'd been sewing and carrying for

Mrs. Charlie all day long decided that come what may she was not going to stand up in the bus on her way home. And she did not. The fightin' and footracin' which ensued resulted in Black folks boycotting the buses in Montgomery (where it began) and other towns. Several bus companies went bankrupt. Charlie began thinking about opening doors!

Against this background Brumsic Brandon's strip becomes even more unique. The cartoonist is actually violating what has always been an American taboo, and that is to create non-white characters or even poor white characters who are human, sympathetic and even lovable. Brandon employs his irresistible humor to level the walls of racism. And what better stage setting could he devise than the schools and the kids they're trying to educate?

In the most recent of the five cartoon books in the *Luther* series, Brandon buses his kids to the Alabaster Avenue Elementary School for their daily duels with Miss Backlash. Nobody gets hurt in these encounters, but the feelings of children both Black and white are so brilliantly expressed that no reader could be unaware of the fact of being educated!

I suspect that Brother Brumsic, like most of us kids, realized that he was being "put on" when our Miss Backlash insisted that the invention of the steam engine—or was it the cotton gin—was the greatest contribution to mankind's progress. All kids know that the most important contribution was the discovery of the sugar-covered laxative. The same as castor oil but, oh man, it tastes so good! Being the talented artist that he is, Brother Brandon simply developed his own sugar-coated brands with names like Luther, Oreo, Mary Frances, Hardcore and, of course, the thoroughly probable Miss Backlash. According to what I hear, Americans from coast to coast are gobbling it up like mad. If only someone had slipped a little taste to, say, Lester Maddox or Earl Butz or even Vice-President Nelson Rockefeller.

Where Is the Justice?

With you, I, an American Negro, am deeply concerned about justice. We care, and rightly so, about the denial of religious liberty of a man in Yugoslavia and about the rights of Jews in Europe. We care that a Chinese peasant shall have the right to till his land free from fear and want. But I ask you this—an honest question—why is there talk of Spain and Yugoslavia, of Palestine and Greece but no talk of Aiken County, South Carolina. Why so little of Isaac Woodard, a veteran whose eyes were gouged out by a policeman's club? Why do we sweep the burning fact of discrimination against 15,000,000 citizens under the carpets of America?

There are 15,000,000 Negro Americans who do not believe you, ladies and gentlemen, when you say, "justice." We have reasons to believe you mean justice for whites only.

Yet (there are many of you who know this), we love America as deeply as any love their country.

The first man to die in the American Revolution was Crispus Attucks, a Negro who fell in the Boston Massacre. From that war to this last war Negroes despaired with America's defeats and gloried with America's victories—for they were our defeats and our victories, too. And, in all American history, there has never been a Negro traitor. We helped plow the fields, build the dams, write the poems and sing the music of America. Are not all Americans proud, of Doree Miller, of Frederick Douglass, of

"Officer, what Alabama bar was you holed up in back in '44 when I was in Normandy protectin' your civil rights?"

Paul Robeson, of Joe Louis, of Marian Anderson? For, you see, we are not people who despair—we are people who, having lived on the edge of life, want simply to live life fully, to live life without barriers, to be all that we can be and a little of what (like you) we hope to be.

Two years ago in the Italian mountains I sat with a group of riflemen of the Negro 92d Division. A sergeant offered me a canteen cup of pineapple juice spiked with a ferocious liquid. He said, "We got to take good care of this egg" (meaning me) "because it's going to take a lot of writing to tell the folks that Sergeant Dixon didn't come over for this hell so his kid would keep getting thrown out of restaurants when he tries to buy a meal." Well, the sergeant was putting an awful lot of weight on this egg, but not nearly as much as the Nazis put on him when he was cut to pieces crossing the Arno.

I think of all the sergeants, the corporals and the privates who were luckier than Sergeant Dixon, the ones who came back. What of them today in America? What do they face in victorious America, with Nazism defeated?

Every soldier who fought put on a uniform and gave up two, three, four years of his life. He worked, he fought, sometimes he bled. Sometimes he lost a limb—but above all, he gave America those years of his life. And America said, "We won't forget you." That's simple justice. Now they're back. Most veterans are bitter men because the simple things they ask—a home, a job, security—they cannot have. But what, I ask, is it like to be a Negro veteran?

You fought, if you are a Negro veteran, to tear down the sign "No Jews Allowed" in Germany, to find in America the sign "No Negroes Allowed." You fought to wipe out the noose and the whip in Germany and Japan, to find the noose and the whip in Georgia and Louisiana. One veteran put it to me this way: "I got through fighting in the E.T.O.," he said, "and now I've got to fight in the S.T.O."

I asked, "What's the S.T.O.?" He said, "Haven't you heard? The Southern Theater of Operations. U.S.A."

There were nearly 1,000,000 Negroes in the service—more than 600,000 of them in labor battalions. We were asked to serve, then told we were not good enough to fight. We can talk, yes, of the Negro divisions—the 92d, say—which suffered over 3,000 casualties, won 12,000 decorations including 1,095 Purple Hearts. We can speak of the Negro Seabees at Iwo Jima, of Negroes building the Lido Road, running the Red Ball Highway, fighting in mixed battalions in the Bulge—but having said this, we have not talked of the most important part: what the Negroes were not allowed to do. For to say it simply, you did not let us offer the blood in our veins to save our own lives and the lives of other men whose skin was white.

And there were other things. Negro men were murdered, yes, by American soldiers, because they broke the law of Jim Crow. When our men met the British and the French, they welcomed us. We became their friends until the American Army set up the American custom of racial hatred on the soil of England.

And what was the cost of this Jim Crow? Not merely that the precious words "America" and "freedom" became suspect in the eyes of the world, but more than that. It cost us lives. Lives of white men, of Frenchmen, Russians and Chinese—because there were many battles in this war when replacements were needed. But the American rule of war was "No Negroes allowed on the front lines" until the 92d finally got there.

I listened to the Axis radio. Tokyo Rose said, and she quoted American sources, that Negroes were good enough to serve in the American Army, but they weren't good enough to pitch in the American Big League baseball. And they broadcast this not only to our own troops but also to the billion and a half colored peoples of the earth.

In Italy I saw leaflets telling the liberated Italian people not to mix with Negroes, for we were brutes who must be kept in our places and it was found that American soldiers, more anxious to maintain Jim Crow than to win victory, had printed and distributed these leaflets.

And then came victory and discharge. There, too, we got the sweepings. You remember some of us were stranded in Europe because, as one captain put it, his ship was not equipped with proper facilities for segregation. So we waited, 3,000 miles from home, until they tacked up the Jim Crow signs aboard our transports. Then we could come home.

I could tell you that of the ninety-seven veterans' hospitals operating at the present time, seventeen do not accept Negro vets except in cases of extreme emergency. Or that for over 3,000 Negro vets in Georgia and Mississippi there is not one available hospital bed. I could tell you that at the U.S.E.S. office in Birmingham, which has not one Negro on its staff, a Negro vet with a master's degree is offered a job as a janitor. I could tell you that since V-J Day more than nine Negro veterans have been lynched and not one of the lynchers brought to justice. But these are facts which can be found filed in reports. I'd rather tell you two simple stories.

In Monroe, Ga., I talked with a Negro veteran who'd served three and a half years in the Aleutians, in Europe and in the Pacific.

Before enlisting, he'd worked for a white family in Monroe, mowing the lawn, serving meals and running errands. His salary was three dollars a week—four dollars some weeks. A day after he returned home discharged, his former employers told him they expected him to appear at work the next morning. He didn't dare refuse, so he said he wanted to rest a while. But they complained they couldn't wait. You see, they'd been inconvenienced by his absence those three-odd years. A few days later he was asked by a bank clerk in the town if he was in trouble. The vet was puzzled. The clerk explained that the employers had been at the bank investigating his account. "If you've stolen money," warned the clerk, "you'd better return it before there's real trouble."

"If they want you to work for them," he said, "they'll get you. When the sawmill operators need men they tip off the police and they arrest a few of us. Next thing you know bail's been paid and you're working at the sawmill for ten dollars a week—minus the bail. They'll get you if they want you."

During the last ten months my work with the NAACP has carried me into the lynch areas several times. Climbing into a Georgia bus, I moved to the rear which is reserved for Negroes. It was hot, so I took off my jacket and put it into the baggage rack. Someone nudged me. It was a squat, blue-eyed Georgian. "Hold my coat, boy," he said. I pretended not to hear him. He nudged me again. "I said, 'hold my coat,'" he repeated. I sensed the sudden stiffening of the Negroes behind me and I carefully turned away, pretending not to have understood. But the man nudged me again. I realized that the white passengers were watching. This time he held out a package of cigarettes.

"Open those cigarettes, boy!" I stood for a long moment staring and decided that no matter what had to happen I was not going to open those cigarettes. "I said, 'open those cigarettes',," he said once more. I looked at the Negro women stiffly sitting behind me and at the three freshly scrubbed kids in their going-to-town clothes. I thought of a world of things in that second. I knew violence stood in that bus—possibly death. And then I felt a gentle tug at my sleeve. Looking down I saw the tired face of an old Negro woman. "Open the cigarettes, son," she said. I turned, took the cigarettes and opened them. He simply grinned. The watching white passengers turned their heads toward the front of the bus and the old Negro woman stared at the floor.

Well, we've been talking of justice . . . justice for Negro vets . . . or justice to 15,000,000 Negroes. I ask . . . rather I demand . . . justice for America. For I believe, with a million Negroes whose shoes left their mark at Kassarine Pass, Cassino, Anzio, Normandy, Berlin, Iwo Jima and Tokyo, that here in this nation of ours we have the heart and the tools for shaping a new world. The tools were left us by men who long ago dreamed the greatest dream ever known to men. They set it down indelibly in our Constitution and left it to be treasured and fought for by the stout hearts they knew our hills and rivers and valleys would produce. And what has happened to our dream of justice? I'm afraid I know. It is being thrown away in measured steps. Steps which have names like Isaac Woodard, the Ferguson brothers, Roger and Dora Malcolm, John and Sarah Dorsey, Snipes, Gilbert, Fletcher, Jones and . . . Do you recognize them? Some of them might have been with you on the beach at Okinawa, but they were killed, instead in America.

We are talking of justice and the agencies of justice. In Columbia, Tenn., where an entire Negro community was subjected to wholesale and vicious vandalism, the Department of Justice was unable to identify a single guilty person. Now, Columbia is a small town where every one knows every one else and yet the same agency that tracked down every foreign spy during the last war, the greatest secret service agency in the world, was unable to find a single clue, locate a single criminal who took part in the crushing of an American community.

In every field of crime, though some escape, criminals are caught—every crime but one. For the crime of race hate and lynching there has never been a conviction in the history of the United States.

But the Department of Justice has acted, some will say, against peonage. Yes, they have acted because, by now, most Americans are convinced that human slavery is evil. But in other fields, some will say, the department's hands are tied by lack of Federal legislation. To me, a layman, an agency committed to defending the lives of its citizens should spend less time finding legal reasons for not acting, and more time acting on behalf of human justice . . . unless—(there is a conclusion I hesitate to draw)—unless there are more than "legalistic" reasons for not acting, unless there is an unwillingness to act.

When we returned home from this war we were certain of one fact. We either had to choose Communism or we had to make democracy work. If only you could realize how desperately people who are not white want to be Americans.

Why I Left America

My very, very dear friends, this is always very difficult for me to stand up and speak because I haven't spoken, really, since 1948 when I was with the NAACP. My best friends here tell me that it hasn't been too bad, so I'll try to go along and tell you about some of the things and explain some of the things that you just heard about me in the introduction. I'm particularly happy that Julia Wright is here tonight because she is working on a biography of her father's life. She's been doing research and I've helped her in the little way that I could. It's going to be an extremely interesting book and I'm very happy that it's going to be published because it will clear up a lot of rumors and other misstatements that have been published in the past.

As you've heard already, I was raised in what is now the "jungle" of New York, the lower Bronx, and, indeed, at that time it was a very pleasant place. We played like all other kids. Where I lived was a very small enclave, a ghetto, but there were a number of ghettos. Most of the people there were immigrants; first generation Americans from Italy, Ireland, Poland, and there were a few French people. In a way, in a peculiar way, it was an integrated community composed of several separated ghettos. That was about the norm in those days. The idea of integration hadn't really gotten started, so I think that for anyone living today it would be a period that would be really difficult to understand. But we played in the woods, we played in

Miss McCoy

the Indian caves, we absorbed some of the beauty that was in that area and it was, I can say, in spite of some of the racism which I began to learn in school, a rather pleasant life.

I wasn't really interested in doing cartoons at that time, but I had one teacher, Miss McCoy, who used to call me and the other Black pupil in the school—a great, big guy by the name of Prince Anderson—to the front of the room and present us to the class. She'd say, "These two, being Black, belong in a waste basket." Well, there was no way of defending oneself against that. So, I began to build up a kind of rage against her. There was no way that I could have gotten back at her because if I had, it would have been much more serious than it turned out. In the end, it turned out rather beneficial to me because I began doing cartoons of Miss McCoy in my notebooks. Needless to say, she never saw any. But they were much more violent than anything you can find in the present day so-called comics. I did her up fine. And it did me an awful lot of good. So much good that I never really hated her. I considered her quite a poor, dumb, sloppy woman who was injecting something into students which I really didn't understand. It was like injecting them with their first "trips" on heroin, or what other drugs there are. They became addicts, most of them. I guess they still are. But to me, it was an opening to a source of pleasure which has remained and sustained me; the art of what we might call, loosely, cartoons.

There are many other incidents I could tell you about from that period, but I suppose it would take up too much of your time. But I don't want to forget about Dougan, the cop. Dougan took part in every parade and carried the flag which swayed with his overfed buttocks along the Grand Concourse where all the parades were held. I imagine I have in my notebooks, if I could find them, portraits of Dougan which would also come under the heading of "vicious" cartoons. He had a bad habit, and that was going on a spree every Saturday night and beating the hell out of every Black kid he could find. One kid was very, very seriously injured and the old Methodist Episcopal minister, who was a friend of mine, used to explain, "Well, Dougan kind of sprained his brain." The boy was partly paralyzed. But that was life in the Bronx.

About the time I was 17 and graduated from high school, I like to say that I ran away from home. I went to Harlem, and that was a most beautiful place where, fortunately for me, I came into, or rather, ran into, the hands of some wonderful people; people who formed an important part of the so-called Black Renaissance. They were people like Langston Hughes, Wally Thurmond, Bud Fisher, all really wonderful writers. I lived in the YMCA where you could rent a room for $2 a week and they put all the regular inhabitants up on the 11th floor. Among them were people like Charlie Drew, who became the developer of blood plasma, distinguished physicians, physics people, and biologists. Now, this was a wonderful experience for me. Charlie Drew had graduated already from McGill University and was experimenting on his own in developing blood plasma. One day, Charlie got a telegram asking him to come down to the British Embassy and it was signed: Winston Churchill. So, Charlie stormed into my room and he said, "Ollie, I know you sent that god-damned telegram!" I swore to him that I hadn't and it took us some time to convince him to at least look into it. So, he did, and they said, "Yes, Dr. Drew, we are waiting for you at the British Embassy." This was right at the time of Dunkerque, and when he got to the Embassy, he learned that this was a perilous time for the British army and what they needed most was blood plasma. So, Charlie flew to London and worked on his blood plasma after having met Churchill, and really performed a magnificent job. He came back to the United States after having developed this whole system of supplying blood, where a draft board tells him to go to the Navy department in Washington. He went there and presented himself, the distinguished Dr. Drew, and they suddenly realized that a very serious error had been made. So, I guess they found someone else to supply the blood plasma, and Charlie Drew became a terribly, terribly embittered man.

I was having trouble with my own draft board. I was working, at that time, on Adam Powell's paper, *The People's Voice*, which I think was a remarkable newspaper. It had really started the whole business about "hire Black," and that sort of thing in Harlem. There was the Cotton Club in Harlem which was owned by gangsters who came uptown each night, and went back downtown each night with the loot, which was considerable. Blacks were not allowed into the Cotton Club as patrons, only as entertainers. There were places like Frank's Restaurant on 125th Street, a marvelous place for steaks, but no Blacks were allowed to enter there, either. So, there was a movement which was started by Adam Powell through *The People's Voice*, his newspaper. At that time I was the art editor and, occasionally, the sports editor. The time came for me to go see my draft board, but I had discovered before I went there that two of the members were very wealthy Wall Street lawyers. My notice to come in to the draft board, however, read: You have been se-lected by a number of your neighbors to . . . etc., etc., etc., and I got inspired and nerved-up. So, I turned to the draft board as they were about to send me off to the butcher shop and I said, "I'm sorry. One moment, please. I'd like to ask you gentlemen a question." I pointed to the lead Wall Street lawyer and I said, "Do you gentlemen live in this neighborhood?" Well, no one had ever heard this in the draft board, so there was a long silence. I happened to look over to a brother, an architect, I've forgotten his name, but he was a leading Harlem architect, and his eye barely winked. Soon I realized I was on the right track. Sure enough, I was told by the draft board to go home and wait. So, as far as service in the armed forces is concerned, I'm still waiting!

I knew that I had strong feelings about the war against fascism. But, I also had strong feelings against fighting in a racially segregated army, and this was a wonderful solution: I became a war correspondent for the *Pittsburgh Courier* then, and later, I was a part of what they called the Armed Forces Pool, which was quite a compliment, really.

And so, I went to north Africa. We were torpedoed on the way. The rudder was shot off and it took us 48 days to get to Taranto, a little place in the "instep" of Italy. There, I remember something happening which appeals to my cartooning side. A few of us went ashore and saw a large group of Black troops standing and ogling, watching these new fellows come in. So, some of the boys said, "What do you know, man? How is it over here?" And these fellows looked, turned to each other and said, "Hoola boola, booga wooga." And I remember one of the cats from Harlem saying, "Well, I'll be damned! They've forgotten how to speak English!" Later, we discovered that they were South African troops.

Off we went to the wars. Some months later, there had been a new program set up by the War Department for inspecting the morale of the Black troops. There was no morale, but they had to inspect what there was. People like Walter White were sent to Europe and Ben Davis, the commander of the 332nd Fighter group, who was a friend of mine, called me in and said, "Look, we've got this on our hands. We have Walter White coming here and I've been told to delegate you to see that he doesn't get hurt." Well, if you know anything about Walter White, you know that he was a very headstrong guy, and I couldn't see how I was going to be able to do that. But I had a Jeep and a driver and I took him around the battlefront. He didn't get hurt, although we were in some very, very tough spots because of his saying, "Well, no, Ollie. Let's go up there and see what's happening there," with shells flying in all directions. He'd say, "Well, man, that's outgoing," and I'd say, "No, no, brother, that's incoming!"

We got back after a couple of weeks in the field and in one of the tents sitting around with some of the flyers, Walter White, who was a wonderful guy, but who had a big ego that you really couldn't handle, turned to the fellows who were sitting around and said, "Look, boys, when we flew over the Bay of Naples there were a number of shots fired and I guess that was a salute for me. Now I think there were 18 shots fired. Tell me, for what rank was that?" And these pilots looked down and said, "Well, Mr. White, they was tryin' to shoot yo' ass down!"

When he got back to the states, I guess as a result of my having kept him alive, he began sending me letters asking me to start a public relations department for the NAACP. Well, I wanted to get back to art when I got back to New York; I had no interest in anything like that. I had an interest, but I didn't think that I was the one for it. If you remember, there was a wave of awful lynchings at that time. You see, a lot of these fellows had bonuses coming from the Army. They had also saved up their salaries because there was no place to spend it. Blacks were not allowed in the Red Cross Clubs, and they had what was called a Liberty Club system. They didn't have very much in the Liberty Club and so you could save all your salary. They would take their money, to the South, especially, and buy a little piece of land. Well, you can see how that would begin to make the system get a little wobbly. The Southerners didn't like that, the idea of Blacks owning their own farms, so they began lynching whole families of Blacks. In one episode, a man by the name of Isaac Woodard was on a bus. He'd come back from the Pacific, got on a bus somewhere in perhaps Louisiana, and was on his way to New York. Having been away in the armed forces for so long, he'd forgotten a lot of the rules, and he was sitting in a seat where he should not have been. Policemen dragged him off the bus in some town, he didn't exactly remember what the name of the town was. They beat him all night in a cell and then gouged both of his eyes out. There was no record in any Red

Cross hospital, or veteran's hospital, and there had to be in a case like that where a veteran was practically killed, but there was no record. No record was ever found. I don't remember exactly how this case came to the attention of the NAACP, but it was at that time that I decided that I would have to take the job.

This was a fantastic incident which really had nation-wide significance. Here was a case, a terrible case, where there was no known assailant, no hospital had any record of him, and he didn't know exactly where it had happened except that he thought that it was in South Carolina. This was the first case that I had at the NAACP. I began trying to dream up the way public relations should be done without any real experience. But, I'd read about that sort of thing. I even had some friends on Madison Avenue and, naturally, they gave me tips. I got in touch with Orson Welles through his agent and we corresponded by telephone every Saturday and he would make a broadcast every Sunday evening. It was a fantastically dramatic and interesting program in which he took the role of somebody out hunting down these men who had committed that crime. As a result, they actually discovered the two policemen who had done this. They were brought up and tried, a very quick trial, and they were acquitted. There was a slight error made, and I suppose it was really a matter of our inexperience. He had named the town as being one of the most popular resorts in South Carolina. As a result, pressure was brought to bear. CBS fired him and they terminated his program. The film industry told him that he was no longer welcome and as a result, he left the United States and never returned.

There were other cases like this and we had spectacular successes. As a result, I was invited to speak at the Herald Tribune Forum in 1946, and one of the people I had to debate with was [Attorney General] Tom Clark. Clark actually named me as a Communist. I had trouble from that time on, but I wasn't worried about my personal situation at all. I was worried about the

NAACP. If it could have been proven that an executive of the NAACP was a Communist . . . well, that was all they wanted. They wanted to push these organizations further to the right and get them out of the way.

I met an old friend at the Hotel Teresa Bar which was one of the most famous and pleasant watering places for the brothers and I said, "Look, come in and have a drink"—I almost mentioned his name and I mustn't do that—and he said, "O.K." So we went in and had some drinks and after a while, I called the bartender and I said, "How much do I owe? I have to leave." And you know how the brothers push each other back and forth saying, "No, man, let me pay this." "No, man, let *me* pay this . . . " Well, somebody's got to come to a decision here. So, while we were doing this, my friend was making funny motions below the bar. I turned back to him and took a closer look. He was showing me his badge . . . Army Intelligence. So I wondered aloud, "Man, my old friend. What's happening?" He said, "I'm warning you to go to Europe. Take a vacation for six months and let this thing blow over." Well, he was much more optimistic than I was when he told me that. So I asked him, "How can you do this? It's a terribly dangerous thing you're doing by telling me this." He said, "Yes, but look," and he held his hand out next to mine. Both hands were black. So that was that. Three weeks later I was on a boat. That was in 1951 and I've stayed in Europe all of that time.

I managed to continue my Bootsie cartoon until 1962 or 1963, when, I think under certain pressures, *The Chicago Defender* told me they had to dispense with my services. I had a week's notice. If you've ever lived in Europe as a Black expatriate, you know that a week's notice could be deadly because I lived on hardly anything, just managed to make it. But, it was a wonderful life, with terribly interesting people. Most of the Blacks who had been demobilized in Europe were on what was then called the GI Bill of Rights which gave them a certain amount of money each month to continue an education, or start an education. I really met some fantastic people in that era, very. There was one fellow, good old Harris, and I met him and he told me, "Look, man, you study art at La Grande Chaumière." That's a big place where artists can go and work all day for about 50 cents a day. And it still exists. It's a wonderful place in the development of French art history. Practically everyone at some time or another had been through La Grande Chaumière. You could have teachers if you wanted to, or you could study on your own.

So, I met old Harris in the Cafe Select, one of the places in Paris, and he said, "Look, man, I'm going to be at the Grande Chaumière. I'm going to be an artist." So I said, "Well, that's alright. That's great." So, sure enough, he showed up. He had asked the brothers, "What do you do when you go to the Grande Chaumière?" "The first thing," he was told, "you buy a beret. Then you get some paper and some charcoal and a board to place on a chair and you watch and do what everybody else is doing," which is what old Harris did. He was so engrossed in preparing himself for this new career that he didn't realize what was happening up in front of him on a stand. This was a normal thing at La Grande Chaumière. I hadn't thought to tell him about it. But the curtains were pushed aside and out stepped a nude model. Now, Harris was from Mississippi. To be suddenly faced with this naked white lady was too much for old Harris. He reached down and slapped his beret on his head and packed up his stuff and flew out of there. It took us a long time to explain the circumstances to Harris and to convince him that there was nothing to it, they weren't trying to trick him. I don't know how far Harris went in his art studies, but this was serious. It made a great difference in Harris' life, I'm sure. He began to develop a completely different perspective on himself, certainly different from that he'd had in Mississippi. I remember later, during a talk, Harris had said to me, "Look, man, the good

Lord showed me a way out of Mississippi and I ain't going to be ungrateful and go back there. Because if I go back there, the last thing I can do is get a job maybe as a waiter at the country club, and who's going to be sitting there at that country club? There's going to be Wernher von Braun, who is the Nazi head of the whole missile program. He's going to be sitting at a table and he's going to say, 'Harris, come over here,' just like he's been doing when he was in the SS." He said, "I ain't giving him that opportunity." And he never did, as far as I know.

I was just telling someone at the dinner table about an African chap I saw in a little cafe, the Monaco Cafe it was called . . . very dark and dingy on a little street, rue de Seine, which goes right down to the Seine river. One afternoon, way in the back, I saw one figure. It was difficult to make him out but I didn't want to sit in an empty place and I walked in there and sat down near him. His back was to the wall. I also saw that he had on a black sweater, a black suit; Africans were cold in Paris and even in summertime they wore these black raincoats, I guess, black socks, black shoes. I didn't get a look at his teeth, but he was a stolid looking fellow and he sat there and I sat near him. Finally, out of the corner of his mouth he said, "Where you from, man?" So, I told him I was from America. "That's what I figured. Been here long?" I told him, no, it was the first time I had been there. He never looked at me and always spoke to me out of the corner of his mouth. So I said, "Look, man, it's dark in here. Why do you sit back here?" He said, "Man, I got no trust." He was sitting there facing that door all the time and he wasn't going to be tricked either, you see. I knew him for years in that place and he never sat in another seat except that one there. Incidentally, I met a couple of young ladies who told me that even his underwear was black. Eventually, he met a young lady from Sweden and she took him to Sweden where someone told me that he lived in a sort of a small castle overlooking the Skagerrak and may still be there.

Why I Left America

Now these were the kinds of wonderful experiences I had with so-called expatriates. Once a fellow said, "Ah, what's all this stuff in the newspapers and magazines? *Time*, *Life*, and *Newsweek* are all doing lots of articles on expatriates." Now, the focus was actually on Black expatriates, you see, and it made a big difference because Hemingway, F. Scott Fitzgerald, all the great American writers were all in Paris at one time or another. But when Black expatriates sort of joined the "fraternity," it wasn't a very popular thing with the authorities in the United States and you can easily see why. These were really disrupting ideas which existed. Blacks had to be held in check. They had to fear white law, and that sort of thing. Living in Paris and having experiences that Blacks shouldn't have was not conducive to a smooth course towards whatever American history would finally produce. So, Blacks were really harrassed by the journalists, American journalists. I remember being interviewed quite a few times and I asked the interviewer who was with *Time* magazine why he was so worried about me being an expatriate, whereas down the street there was the American library where Hemingway hung out. Faulkner spent time there. Every American writer spent time there. But when Blacks showed up, why, it became something else. Well, you can see that clearly, this was a continuing motif in our way of life. I understand it has improved. I hope so. I understand that the conditions here have improved. I dearly hope so.

If I had been able to, I would have come back to America because my roots are in America. That wasn't possible and I couldn't say that I have been too uncomfortable. But one of the most distinguished expatriates and a focus of attention was Richard Wright whom I considered one of the greatest American writers, a guy who started in Mississippi with no education—that in itself is a wonder. He went to Chicago, came to New York, and wound up in Paris as a literary stellar star. He was admired and worshipped by the French people until his death in 1960. I would say that Dick was my closest friend. We had a small group, Dick Wright, Chester Himes and myself and we lived and enjoyed French life. I would say that if you had to live anywhere in Europe without a passport, France was the place. I'm not saying that racism doesn't exist in France. It certainly does. But it's not oppressive. One is never harrassed racially by a Frenchman. A Frenchman has too much dignity to walk up behind you in the street and call you a dirty nigger. That wouldn't enter the mind of a Frenchman and he might just be a racist. Since then, things have changed very much. At the end of the Algerian War a lot of the Algerian plantation owners moved to France. They were called "Pieds Noirs," black feet. They really were people who had black minds because they have injected the worst kind of racism into France where Algerians, for the most part, were lynched. I see Julia nodding her head; she knows better than I. She's been living there all her life. The anti-Algerian feeling is very, very intense and this, as racism always does, has infected the whole French atmosphere, I think, so that racism is much more open and apparent now than it was then.

In 1961 after Dick died, I went to Berlin to talk with publishers about illustrating American and English classics like Irving, Conrad, and other outstanding writers of the early period and while I was there, in August, I heard a very sinister sound in the streets. I looked out of my tiny hotel window and down below there was a stream of tanks going along. They were Soviet tanks. That gave me a bad feeling because I'd seen that before.

I went down out of my room and walked in the direction the tanks were going for about a mile. On the edge of a place which has since become known as Checkpoint Charlie there was a line of US tanks. I knew I was right in the middle of World War III. I had had enough of wars and I didn't want to be in the middle of any war after that. So, I went back to my hotel, but found that I couldn't leave because I didn't have the proper visas. The bureaucracy, the cold war bureaucracy had really set in at that point. I was a virtual prisoner. I couldn't leave there. I lost my French apartment, I lost everything. I had to stay there. I must say that it hasn't been too unfortunate or uncomfortable because I had an opportunity to start this line of political cartoons using color which had been entirely different from what I'd been doing. Gradually, I was published in the top satirical magazines in the GDR and I've been doing that ever since 1961. There were great temptations to leave there, but I liked the work. I continued to work and I've been there ever since. I maintained, loosely, some relationships with a young lady I really consider a daughter who is now working on a biography of her father's very fantastic life and the circumstances of his death, which are still very unclear. I was asked by *Ebony* magazine to write an article about that. I certainly didn't make any charges, although I've had certain suspicions, but I tried to inject into that article that this wasn't the end of the story. It should be looked into. And I'm very happy to say that that feeling has spread. I've never met a Black person who did *not* believe that Richard Wright was done in. By whom, I don't know. I've no idea. There are so many possibilities. But, you'll probably read of them in Julia's book. That's about all I have to say. Thank you.

Index

Index

Index